Surgery in Turbulent Mesopotamia

Erbil's Citadel

Amir Al-Dabbagh

Surgery in Turbulent Mesopotamia

*Work and Life in Erbil, Iraq,
one of the most Ancient Cities
on Earth*

AMIR AL-DABBAGH

THE CHOIR PRESS

First published in the United Kingdom in 2021 by
The Choir Press

ISBN 978-1-78963-245-3

In memory of my brother,
Salam, everlasting in his family's hearts.

Salam, at graduation

To my father, my first and greatest inspiration.

To my mother, the first and most genuine everlasting source of love.

To my family, wife Afaf, and three children, Wisam, Raed and Sandra.

Contents

Acknowledgements

My deepest gratitude is to my dear colleague and friend, Professor Munthir Al-Doori, whose advice and comments on the initial manuscript of this book were extremely useful. Munthir's readiness to help and support others knows no boundaries at all.

Introduction

Back to Erbil, My Hometown, 26 Years Later

In his book The Art of Loving,[1] a best seller, the German psychologist Erich Fromm describes different forms of love in a most objective, humanistic, and analytic style. In all aspects of love, he describes the most vital element inherent in the activity, saying: 'Love is a power which produces love; it is the active concern for the life and growth of that which we love.'

I have been thinking, for several years, of starting to write this vital chapter of my autobiography. There was so much in my mind, accumulated throughout my experience as a general surgeon mainly in Erbil, Iraq, that I was eager to put in words. It wasn't just the clinical and educational aspects of my work in Erbil as a general surgeon and clinical lecturer which I extremely enjoyed, but there was something else as great and precious, pushing me to start writing up this memoir as well as pulling me back to return to Erbil.

That was simply, but most vitally, the genuine trust and the strong professional and friendly relationships built with the people, colleagues, and students in this great city during the 14 years of work from April 1980 to November 1993.

Again, having become familiar with the structure of the health service in the United Kingdom, and the well-organised system of delivery of health services all over the country, I became increasingly interested in finding the best way of

---

[1] *The Art of Loving.* Erich Fromm, Thorsons Edition 1995

co-operating with my colleagues in Erbil to help improving the structure and delivery of health services, particularly in surgery, in Kurdistan and all over Iraq.

The other reason, as became clear to me during my visits to Erbil in May and November 2019, is the fact that only very few people in Erbil were aware of the real reason behind my sudden departure from Erbil in November 1993. I felt this was another strong obligation on me to explain the facts as they happened.

Since I started working again in the UK in 1995, and especially following my appointment as a consultant surgeon at Trafford General Hospital in Manchester in 2001, I kept looking for the opportunity to go back to Kurdistan.

This first happened in 2002 when invited to attend a surgical congress in the city of Duhok, northwest of Erbil, and to chair surgical sessions. It was a great occasion, though for a short period of time, only eight days. My whole family and a large number of close relatives travelled from Baghdad to Duhok, some 500 kilometres to the north, to see me as it was almost ten years following my forced departure from Erbil in November 1993.

Encircled by mountains along the Tigris river, Duhok is a beautiful city in Iraqi Kurdistan and its tourist industry is rapidly growing.

I met with several of my colleagues and previous students from Erbil and Sulaymaniyah (a major city to the northeast in Iraq) attending the same meeting. I didn't then travel to Erbil mainly because the situation and circumstances weren't conducive at that time.

My second return to Kurdistan, to Erbil, was in the year 2012 with my wife. I had then firmly decided to apply for resumption of my appointment as a consultant general surgeon and senior clinical lecturer at the medical college. I met with the dean of the college, Dr Ali Al-Dabbagh,[2] a consultant general surgeon, and presented my formal application for re-employment. We stayed 12 days at that time in a hotel in Erbil and had a great time with so many colleagues and friends. It took only few days before many people realised I was back, and that was followed by daily invitations during the rest of our stay, which were extremely hard to decline.

During this visit, I could clearly see the significant changes that have taken place all over the city of Erbil, with signs of modern construction everywhere.

Dr Ali Al-Dabbagh passed my application to the president of the University of Salahuddin, after confirming his approval.[3] He informed me that it would take few weeks to get the final approval. Obviously, I needed more than that time to apply for retirement from my job in Manchester and sort few things out.

We left Erbil, my wife to Canada and I back to Manchester. I received, a few weeks later, an email from Dr Ali Al-Dabbagh

---

[2] The surname 'Al-Dabbagh' in the Middle East, describes a profession of the ancestors in the leather industry, which was very popular during the wars. In other words, and akin to many surnames in the UK, it's never been a first name. Dr Ali and I are from different Al-Dabbagh families, entirely un-related.

[3] Named in memory of the historical worrier Salahuddin, known in Western literature as Saladin, the Islamic ruler of the 12th century who commanded massive forces, fought the Europeans and won battles against the crusaders, for the control of the Holy Lands in Palestine; Jerusalem. He started a new Islamic Empire that would reshape the world and ended up actually improving relationships between Europe and West Asia.

confirming the approval of my re-employment.[4] I emailed back, thanking him, and letting him know about some unavoidable delay before returning back to Erbil.

Things didn't go right in 2013, with a major armed conflict having started and spread fast in the north of Iraq and adjacent Syria, which forced me then to change my plans.

My third return to Erbil was in May 2019, having been invited to a major medical congress. I flew to Erbil from Manchester through Doha, Qatar, landing in Erbil's international airport on the 2 May 2019. As I was driven from the airport to my sister's house, I would have never have recognised that this was the same city which I left 26 years back.

The streets, buildings, apartments, major highways, modern housing complexes, shops, supermarkets, etc. were not much different from what you see in a European city. A significant part of the Old City had been demolished and re-structured, so much so that I could hardly know where I was and find my way from one place to another. My sister, Zuvart, and her two daughters, Farah and Maryam, have settled in Ainkawa since 2013. Ainkawa is a suburb of Erbil located some eight kilometres northwest downtown Erbil. Ainkawa is predominantly populated by Assyrians, most of whom adhere to the Chaldean Catholic Church.

This visit was again for a short period of time, just a week. The whole congress took place at Divan's hotel, one of the most beautiful and glamorous hotels in Erbil.

Attendance at this congress was excellent. Specialists in

---

[4] Dr Ali Al-Dabbagh was promoted to the academic position of professor in general surgery in 2015.

different fields in medicine and surgery from different countries were invited as speakers, presenting various topics. I was delighted to find out that most of the prominent speakers were specialists from Erbil, Sulaymaniyah, Baghdad and other cities in Iraq. Specialists in various fields in medicine and surgery included speakers from North American and European countries, as well as from Turkey, Middle-Eastern and Asian countries. I delivered a couple of surgical presentations on some common problems and chaired a session.

The congress was a great success and received lots of compliments and admiration for the excellent organisation.

This visit was the main motivation to return back to Erbil for a longer period of time, a few months later.

I went back to Erbil in November 2019, having received an invitation from my colleagues in October 2019, while still working in Manchester, to deliver some presentations to postgraduate students in surgery. That was for the whole month of November. I am grateful here to Dr Saleem Saeed Qadir and Dr Sadiq Aziz, both specialists in general surgery, for this invitation. I applied for the professional leave to my clinical director at the Manchester Royal Infirmary Hospital (MRI), the main university teaching hospital in Manchester, not expecting to be granted the leave for the whole month, but my situation and the reasons for the leave were fully respected and the leave was granted.

After settling into my sister's house for a day, I started making phone calls with my colleagues to organise a programme for the presentations, as planned. The organisation for the delivery of my presentations to the postgraduate students was excellent. These presentations were held in different hotels in Erbil and were attended also by a large number of consultant colleagues. I can only compliment and congratulate the organisational committee for all the work and effort involved, particularly to Dr Saleem Qadir.[5]

I also attended several surgical meetings held regularly and weekly at the two teaching hospitals, where various general surgical problems are presented and discussed and were well attended by under and postgraduate students as well as consultants. These meetings were organised and supervised by my colleague, Professor Nooraddin Ismail, with excellent record of attendance.

It didn't take longer than a week or ten days when I started feeling the warmth of reception, not just from my colleagues and previous medical students, most of whom have become specialists in different medical specialties, but also from the society and people of Erbil. I wouldn't be exaggerating at all saying that a great majority of people in their mid-50s and above whom I met during these two visits still remembered me and were so happy to see me back again. It wasn't just remembering my name and that I once worked in Erbil, but it was the gratitude, respect and love they still felt towards me after all these years that moved me so much.

It was this reception which was enough to make me feel again how vital that part of my life in Erbil was. Having worked in one of the most historical cities on Earth for almost 14 years, Erbil has taught me so much that I'll remain grateful to, forever.

It never crossed my mind when I first started working in

---

[5] Dr Saleem Qadir is currently the president of the Kurdistan Board of Medical Specialties (KBMS).

Erbil in 1980 that my non-stop hard work and dedication to my patients and students was gradually and steadily building up such a strong feeling of appreciation, respect and love, which remained alive in their memories so many years later.

And so it happened that my initial intention to start writing this book was further motivated and strengthened again by this experience of recognition and loving reception by the society of Erbil and by my colleagues and previous students, in spite of having been away for 26 years.

Just to add here that I was so pleased to perceive, clearly, how safe and secure living and working in Erbil and rest of Kurdistan has become. The city was very busy all day and night with people enjoying all the facilities in the city.

PART ONE:

Family Relocation, Work and Life

CHAPTER ONE

Forced Departure from Erbil, November 1993

On Friday 12 November 1993, after having finished breakfast with my family in our house at the university housing campus in Erbil, then called 'Zanco's Village', my wife and I were thinking about visiting some friends in the city. It was only few minutes later that our thoughts were interrupted by the doorbell. I went out to find a man and a few women at the door, soon recognising the man as being the son of the owner of the building where I have rented my private clinic. Some of the ladies were in tears, while the man looked very distressed and pleaded to me to rush to the main teaching hospital to operate on his brother, who was urgently admitted due to multiple bullet injuries.

Friday used to be the only holiday of the week in Iraq, and it happened that I wasn't on-call for emergency admissions that particular Friday according to the hospital rota for covering emergency care. However, it never worked out that way in Erbil or any other city in Iraq, and if patients or relatives arrived at our doors any day and at any time, pleading for help, then we would most likely oblige.

I drove my car to the hospital and found the injured patient (who was around 35 years of age) critically unwell with breathing difficulty and evidence of upper abdominal and lower-left chest injuries caused by two bullet entries.

Having dealt with so many injuries during the unfortunate

eight years of the Iraq–Iran War, accumulating vast experience and confidence in dealing with different types of injuries and trauma; I decided to take the patient straight to theatre as any prior investigations might worsen his condition by the delay. In theatre, with blood transfusion already started, I proceeded to open his upper abdomen and initially evacuated large amounts of blood and clots. The injuries were multiple, including the spleen, which was shattered by the bullet injury, two large holes in the stomach, and a large tear in the left diaphragm associated with a fracture of one of the lower ribs. The spleen was removed, and the other injuries repaired. The two bullets were close to each other behind the stomach and were easily removed.

The patient stayed in the intensive care unit for four days and was very stable when transferred to the general surgical ward on the 16 November.

That same day, and while I was in my private clinic around 5 o'clock in the afternoon, my secretary, Mr Mutasim, came to inform me that there was a personal phone call for me to take at our next-door neighbour's barber's workshop. I had no telephone in my own clinic. I went to answer the call. The voice on the other side of the line was abrupt and quick, telling me that I had done them (the people who shot that man) a great harm by saving that man's life, and that I had only 24 hours to leave Kurdistan – otherwise I would be risking my life. I tried to explain that I was just doing my duty as a surgeon, but the voice kept interrupting me and reminding me also that I wasn't the on-call surgeon that day and that I shouldn't have gone to the hospital to treat the man they shot. His tone and threatening style were so aggressive, reminding me that no form of protection and body guarding would save my life if I didn't comply with his orders and leave Kurdistan within 24 hours. He hung up straight after that.

I had no time to waste after that. My personal secretary, Mr Mutasim, advised that we should go immediately to ask the advice of some people he knew in the city. I apologised to the patients and their relatives, who were sat waiting to see me in the clinic, explaining that it was an urgent family matter. Mr Mutasim and I went straight to the office of the mayor of the city, who, after understanding what happened, explained to me the complexity of the conflict leading to the attempted assassination of the person I operated on and saved his life. The person who was shot was apparently a very important political personality, and would have been a target for assassination by a number of groups. The mayor kindly offered me a few options, including the provision of personal bodyguards on a daily basis in Erbil or, if I declined that offer, to provide me with full protection leaving Kurdistan in the direction I preferred.

Again, there was no time to waste. I thanked the mayor for his help, explaining that having bodyguards around me during my daily busy work in Erbil was not really practical, nor sensible, given my position and the reciprocal respect and trust I had built with the society of Erbil.

Subsequent to that we went to see another gentleman whom Mr Mutasim knew as well, for further opinion. His advice was similar to the mayor's, hence I thanked him as well and apologised once more that I couldn't accept the provision of personal protection with bodyguards, for the same reason. I accepted the support and offer from both gentlemen to provide me with the help to escort me and my family towards the borders with Turkey early the following morning.

4

I was very grateful to Mr Mutasim for his support and went back home straightaway and explained the situation to my wife. I told my three children (Wisam ten years, Raed nine years, and Sandra four years) that we were leaving to Turkey the following day for a visit to my dear friend Dr Waleed Khalid (Velit Halit, as known in Turkey) and his family in Ankara.

The time was around 8 o'clock in the evening and while my wife informed several of our neighbours in Zanco's Village about the developments, I rang my friends Kaka Jihan,[6] Kaka Salar, Mr Farook as well as Mr Mutasim who all readily came down to our house. A very dear friend and experienced theatre nurse, Hamdiya, had already heard the news and she came also to our house along with two surgical colleagues, Dr Nazad Khasraw and Dr Nooraddin Ismail.

We all started packing up many suitcases with the absolute essentials we needed to take out with us. This obviously included, besides my wife's and children's belongings, my precious collection of medical slides and some essential books and surgical journals.

On the early morning of Wednesday the 17 November, at around 5 o'clock, two Land Rover cars arrived at our house. Suitcases and all belongings were packed up and the journey to the Kurdish small town of Zakho, on the Turkish border, started just about an hour later. The weather at that time of the year, in the north of Iraq, is usually quite nice, and the journey went smoothly on road, made more interesting and enjoying by having to cross a small river on board of a large, flat, rigid, wooden kayak.

---

[6] The word 'Kaka', preceding the person's name, is an alternative for 'Mr' in the Kurdish language, informally addressing a friend.

My wife and I were quite relieved that our children fully enjoyed the whole journey, in spite of the fact that a good stretch of the roads were unpaved at that time. The beauty of nature on the outskirts of cities in Kurdistan, surrounded by mountains and hills and green landscapes, is always a delight to enjoy seeing any time of the year. The journey to Zakho lasted around five hours.

We stayed one night in Zakho, as the whole family was exhausted by then. I spoke to Dr Waleed Khalid early the next morning; explaining to him what happened and that we were on our way to Ankara.

We crossed the borders into the Turkish city of Silopi on the morning of Thursday the 18 November. We went on a coach trip from Silopi to Ankara, which took almost 17 hours. My wife and I were just so pleased again to observe how lively and delighted our children were, just watching the roads most of the time. As usual, the long trip was interrupted a few times by short stops to enjoy some refreshments.

As expected, Dr Waleed Khalid was waiting for us at the coach station in Ankara, and drove us to his house, which was within a beautiful building complex called 'Konut Kent' on the outskirts of the city.

We spent seven to ten days with Waleed and his family. Waleed's three daughters (Yasemin, Esil and Sevsen) were great friends, almost siblings to my younger two sons and daughter. This goes back to the years where we lived almost as neighbours in Zanco's Village in Erbil for more than eight years.

The weather was beautiful, and we all felt as if we were enjoying a lovely holiday in the aftermath of very stressful and unexpected circumstances.

After staying with Waleed and his family for one week, we

moved to the main city of Ankara where we rented a house. My initial visit to the UK embassy in Ankara, and attempts to apply for immigration to the UK, were not successful as the regulations regarding a whole family's immigration were very difficult at that time.

We made an appointment then to visit the Canadian embassy to apply for immigration. This fortunately happened a few days later. I was advised by the immigration officer, during the interview, that it might prove very difficult for me to be licenced as a surgeon in Canada because of the difficult licencing regulations as applied particularly in surgery.

Our main purpose then was to get our children to resume their school education; hence we accepted the risk, though still hoping that I might eventually be able to pass some basic qualifying exams and possibly some retraining prior to obtaining the Canadian licence to practice surgery.

Dr Waleed knew Professor Dr Ihsan Dogramaci, a professor of paediatric medicine, very well and managed to arrange for a meeting, visiting him in his place in Ankara.[7]

The meeting with Professor Dogramaci went quite well. He listened carefully while I was explaining the circumstances

---

[7] A renowned professor of paediatrics, Ihsan Dogramaci was the executive director and president of the International Paediatric Association and an international leader of educational development. He was born in Erbil in the year 1915, which was then under the Ottoman Empire. He was the founder of Haceteppe University, one of the overall highest ranked universities in Turkey, which specialises in medical sciences in Ankara, and Bilkent University, a leading private university. He was also a chairman of the UNICEF (United Nations International Children's Emergency Fund) executive board, founding president of the Council of Higher Education of Turkey, and he had been the first president and the chairman of its board of trustees in the WHO (World Health Organisation) since 1985.

which led to my forced departure from Erbil and outside the country. He then spoke to his colleague, the president of Istanbul University, recommending me to work at Gerrah Pasha Medical School as a clinical lecturer in the department of clinical anatomy.[8]

---

[8] Dr Waleed himself was subsequently promoted to the academic degree of professor in cardiovascular surgery in 2002.

CHAPTER 2

Life and Work in Istanbul

We moved down to Istanbul a few days later, where I rented an apartment in Atakoy, which is a quarter of Bakirkoy district in Istanbul and very close to the Marmara Sea.

Istanbul is a major city in Turkey that straddles Europe and Asia across the Bosphorus Strait. Its Old City reflects cultural influences of the many empires that once ruled there. In the Sultanahmet district, the open air, Roman-era Hippodrome[9] was for centuries the site of chariot races,[10] and Egyptian obelisks also remain.[11] The iconic Byzantine Hagia Sophia (Turkish 'Ayasofya') was built in the sixth century under the direction of the Byzantine emperor Justinian I.[12]

---

[9] The Hippodrome of Constantinople was an arena used for chariot racing throughout the Byzantine period. First built during the reign of Roman emperor Septimius Severus in the early third century CE, the structure was made more grandiose by emperor Constantine I in the fourth century CE. The Hippodrome was also used for other public events such as parades, public executions and the public shaming of enemies of the emperor. Following the Fourth Crusade in the early 13th century, the Hippodrome fell out of use and its spectacular monuments and artworks were looted.

[10] Chariot racing, in the ancient world, was a popular form of contest between small, two-wheeled vehicles drawn by two, four, or six-horse teams. Such races were a prominent feature of the ancient Olympic Games and other games associated with Greek religious festivals.

[11] An obelisk is a stone rectangular pillar with a tapered top forming a pyramidion, set on a base, erected to commemorate an individual or event and honour the gods.

[12] The building reflects the religious changes that have played out in the region over the centuries, with the minarets and inscriptions of Islam as well as the mosaics of Christianity.

I joined the teaching staff at Gerrah Pasha Medical School two days later and started almost straight away, teaching clinical anatomy and embryology to students in their third year, around 50 in number, assigned to the English section of medical education. Approximately some other 400 students in the same school studied medicine in Turkish language.

Teaching clinical anatomy and embryology to third-year medical students gave me the great opportunity to refresh my knowledge of these subjects and teach them with relevance to clinical application in surgery. My collection of a wealth of slides on surgical problems relevant to my surgical practice in Erbil was of great support to teaching clinical anatomy by the integrated approach. I was also involved in assessing the students during their final examination.

It was also a great opportunity for me to start learning the basics of the Turkish language and I purchased a self-teaching course for that purpose. Turkey is such a beautiful country, with a rich historical background and unparalleled tourist sites anywhere in the world. We had such a great time being close to the Marmara Sea, particularly when the weather became warm starting in March 1994 and rather hot during summertime.

I soon realised also that two doctors, whom I knew very well, were working as specialists in Istanbul. Tahsin was previously my student at the medical college, University of Salahuddin in Erbil, and graduated during the time I was the dean of the college. Shamil, his brother, graduated a year earlier from the medical college in Mosul.

Dr Tahsin (radiologist) and Dr Shamil (orthopaedic surgeon) were soon with us following a phone call. We had a great time with them. They soon became addicted to my wife's cooking and would never miss certain meals, at any price. The traditional Iraqi dishes like bamia, makloba and dolma, cooked exceptionally tasty by my wife, were cooked almost every week to entice them to join us; and they surely always obliged!

Quite often we would enjoy the meals by the side of the Marmara Sea, which was within walking distance from the apartment; hence enjoying the scenic views of the sea as well.

This reminds me also of an interesting incident when I stupidly challenged my wife that I can cook rice as well as she does, if not better. The judges were Tahsin and Shamil. My wife and I cooked rice separately for the tasting challenge. I failed miserably as I mistook sugar, of very fine quality, for salt, and when tasting it before serving and realising what I had done I just added a lot of salt to mask the sweet taste. That surely didn't work, though both Tahsin and Shamil, exchanging interesting silent comments and looks between them, didn't wish to disappoint me and tried hard to approve my cooking style!

Interestingly, it was sometime in early February 1994 when I received a phone call in our rented apartment in Atakoy, and the person calling was the man I operated on due to bullet injuries in Erbil in November 1993. He told me that he got my number from a mutual friend in Erbil.

Apparently, he had tried to leave Kurdistan earlier but couldn't make it until a few days ago. He explained that he was scared and certain that he would be targeted again by the same people who tried to kill him previously. He asked me to provide him with a letter addressed to 'whom it may concern', highlighting the attempt on his life on the 12 November 1993 and that he needed major surgery for that. He desperately needed this document as he was applying for immigration to one of the Western countries or Australia through the UNHCR (United Nations High Commissioner for Refugees).

He came down to the apartment the following day. He surely expressed his gratitude again for saving his life. After a little chat and a cup of tea, I couldn't then resist the temptation to ask him about the attempt on his life and whether he knew the persons who shot him. He apologised that he didn't know who they were or who were behind the attempt. However, I had a strong feeling that he was reluctant to divulge any information in that respect, since all his family were still living in Erbil and he preferred to keep it all confidential. I provided him with the document he needed. I surely didn't see him again after that!

Both Shamil and Tahsin kept visiting us regularly, and they were very much attached to our children as well, particularly Sandra, who was five years of age then.

The day arrived, the 28 July 1994, when we boarded the flight to Toronto, Canada, from Istanbul International Airport. We said farewell to Shamil and Tahsin in the airport. They were in tears.

During the eight months of living in Turkey I managed to spend some time, every day, teaching Wisam and Raed English, as well as some mathematics.

Sandra was only five years then and her progress in Canada was perfect, as expected.

CHAPTER 3

Immigration to Canada

We settled initially in Kitchener, a city in southeast Ontario, the second largest province in Canada.

The city of Kitchener voted in May 1916 to change the name of the city from its original name, Berlin, primarily because of some anti-German sentiment during the First World War. It was renamed Kitchener after Herbert Kitchener, a British Empire field marshal, killed during the war.

Settling in Kitchener did take some time, particularly for our children, getting exposed to a different society and culture, having to cope with their school education. This, however, didn't take any length of time, given their young age. Both Wisam and Raed were assessed by Canadian teachers in August 1994 and were placed at an equivalent year at school, similar to Canadian students of their age.

I remember a situation with Raed, my second son, which happened only a few days after starting his school. He was nine years of age at that time. He came back home that day, in tears, demanding that we go back immediately to Erbil. I couldn't think of the reason behind that, until he told me that he was finding it difficult to understand every word said by his teachers and wasn't sure that he would get good marks at exams. In Erbil, Raed was the top in his class, hence he was feeling very frustrated now.

Wisam, on the other hand, coped extremely well right from the start and he was well-known for his remarkable memory.

I spent almost nine months in Kitchener, Canada, corresponding with most of the medical boards and royal colleges in different Canadian provinces, posting my CV and hoping to get some sort of a quick entry into a retraining programme in surgery anywhere in Canada. Unfortunately, this didn't work out. The quickest pathway back to practicing medicine in Canada was to pass some licencing exams to qualify as a family physician. I could have never accepted that, as surgery was my life, hence I had no choice but to return to the UK.

I managed to contact a very dear colleague and friend of mine, Dr Farhad Omar Huwez, who was working as a registrar in medicine in Glasgow, UK, at that time and explained to him my situation. It wasn't long before I received a call from a medical locum agency in England offering me a locum position for a couple of months as a registrar in the accident and emergency (A&E) department at Wythenshawe hospital in Manchester. Dr Farhad Huwez had obviously recommended me to this agency.[13]

Briefly, I came to know Farhad in Erbil during the years I worked there. Highly esteemed and a very prominent physician, Farhad was very well-known within the medical community in Erbil. His high prestige in society was largely upheld based not just on his knowledge and skills in medicine but also on his ethical principles and his great interest in teaching. He was always available as a colleague, working together.

It's my pleasure again to express my sincere gratitude to Dr Farhad for expediting my return to the UK.

---

[13] Dr Farhad Huwez was subsequently promoted to the academic position of professor of geriatric medicine at New Vision University, and currently consultant stroke physician at the Royal London Hospital.

These nine months which I initially spent living with the family in Canada were very useful, particularly for supporting my children's' education. Needless to say that my wife, Afaf, had the much more important responsibility of bringing up our three children, particularly when they started their school education, not forgetting the significant changes in their life and culture and helping them to cope with all that. She had absolutely no time available to try any recertification requirements to practice medicine in Canada.

The only relative I had in Canada at that time was my cousin, Suad, a very experienced theatre sister in surgery, and her husband, Garabet, a highly skilled radiographer. They had emigrated from Baghdad, Iraq, in 1969 and settled in Richmond Hill, a beautiful city which is part of the Greater Toronto Area. They had three children and we visited them many times while I was still in Canada.

It was the time when Sandra became very fond of their little dog, a puppy named 'Raki', and eventually managed to persuade us to buy her a similar breed in the year 2001, which she also named as 'Raki'

Interestingly, arriving in Canada at the end of July, we were rather surprised to experience a real summertime, with the temperature around 35–37 centigrade. We always had in our minds that the weather in Canada is so cold with lots of snow, so much so that we never expected the opposite. We even thought that friends in Iraq and Turkey were exaggerating about it, until wintertime was upon us and we had to buy lots of new clothes in order to cope with below-freezing temperatures between -5 to -20, and lots and lots of heavy snow for almost five months!

CHAPTER 4

Back to England

I returned to England in May 1995, and after the end of the brief locum post at the A&E department at Wythenshawe hospital I held the position of senior registrar in general surgery in different hospitals in London and Nottingham.

It was only in late 1996 that I came to know that Mr Munthir Al-Doori, a very dear friend of mine with whom I worked at the grade of senior house officer (SHO) in surgery in the Medical City Teaching Hospital in Baghdad (MCTH) back in 1974–1976, was working as a consultant general and vascular surgeon in Huddersfield Royal Infirmary (HRI), Yorkshire, England.

I was then working in Nottingham Queen Medical Centre in England as a senior registrar in endocrine surgery. After a brief chat with Munthir on the phone, he came down to Nottingham few days later.

To this day and forever, I will always remain grateful to Munthir for his support and guidance. He helped me initially to work with him in the position of senior registrar at the HRI for nine months, mainly in the field of vascular surgery where Munthir was the senior consultant surgeon in that department.[14]

---

[14] Professor Munthir Al-Doori graduated from Baghdad's medical college in 1971. He settled in the UK since 1977. His contributions to the health service, particularly in vascular surgery, are well documented. He held important positions as regional advisor on vascular surgery at Yorkshire

Following that, Munthir fully supported me to get back into retraining as a senior registrar in several general surgical specialties for three and a half years within the Yorkshire Surgical Specialist Training Programme. This new structured surgical training program was introduced in the UK in 1993 by the chief medical officer in England, Sir Kenneth Calman.

This program changed the shape and structure of training and assessment from a time-based, apprenticeship-style model, to a more objective workplace-based assessment model. The so-called 'exit exam' is implemented during the final years of the program. Successful completion of the training program and passing the exit exam were absolute requirements for entry in the GMC Specialist Register and applying for consultant posts anywhere in the UK. I passed this examination in July 2000.

It's beyond the scope of this book to provide the full details of this program and the assessment methods. The details are available online for the reader to access if so wished.[15]

Deanery, and was an elected member to the council of the vascular society. He held several positions in different committees within the General Medical Council (GMC). Besides, he regularly contributed to delivery of courses, workshops and assessment of all levels of students in several countries in the Middle East. He received several awards in the UK for his teaching and contributions to medical students' education. He organised communications between universities and scientific bodies in countries like Sharjah, Egypt and Libya with the University of Leeds. His vital contributions to research and surgical aspects on carotid artery disease achieved both national and international recognition. Professor Munthir Al-Doori remains very active in writing and publications and his most recent publication was in the BMJ on 13 September 2019 (Acute Leg Ischemia: Can they wiggle their toes?)

[15] In 1995, the Calman-Hine report on re-structuring cancer services was the first comprehensive cancer report to be produced in the UK and set out

Trafford General Hospital.
Photo © Bill Boaden (cc-by-sa/2.0)

I started working as a consultant general surgeon late 2000, initially in Coventry, near Birmingham, for one year, following which I settled in Manchester, where I am still working at Trafford General Hospital (TGH).[16]

Merger with the Manchester Royal Infirmary (MRI), the largest university teaching hospital in the northwest of

principles for cancer care and the clinical organisation for cancer delivery. It advocated a change from a generalist model (e.g. care given by general surgeons and physicians) that was supported by specialists, to a fully specialist service. The report was widely accepted throughout the UK, though full implementation and centralization of cancer services took few years to materialise.

[16] First built in 1926, the hospital was then named 'Park Hospital'. The hospital was used by the armed forces from September 1939 during World War II initially as a British military hospital. In 1943, the hospital was then transferred to the US army, becoming the tenth US station hospital and treating service personnel from across the world. On the 5 July 1948, Park Hospital became the first NHS hospital in the UK, and the first hospital in the world to offer free healthcare to all. In 1988, Park Hospital was renamed Trafford General Hospital in celebration of the 40th anniversary of its opening.

England, took place in late 2013 and my duties were divided between the two hospitals.

As before, I remained very keen to pursue my interest in undergraduate medical education and was granted the position of undergraduate tutor (UGT) at TGH from 2002 until the end of 2013, when merger with the MRI took place.

I was responsible for supervising the training program of medical students, years three to five from Manchester Medical School, but mainly with supervision, training, and teaching year five students, which is the final undergraduate year. The position of UGT in a district general hospital, as was the case with TGH until late 2013, is similar to the position of a hospital dean in a large university teaching hospital.

During all these years at TGH and the MRI, I became closely involved with the new system of medical education, so-called problem-based learning (PBL), built on the same system of medical education which was started, for the very first time in the world, at the medical school of McMaster University in Hamilton, Canada, in the mid-1960s.

Working back again in the UK, since 1995, has been of great benefit to me from different aspects. Lots of

With Professor Munthir Al-Doori, in Huddersfield.

19

things have changed, though the structure and basics of the National Health Service (NHS) have remained much the same.

The system of annual 'Appraisal' of every single doctor in the country, regardless of their grade and specialty, was implemented first around the year 2000. Revalidation, at five yearly intervals, was first launched in 2012.[17]

---

[17] The details of both appraisal and revalidation can be accessed on the GMC website. Briefly, the principles of appraisal cover the important aspects of the GMC 'Good Medical Practice' (GMP), which addresses mainly the various elements relevant to 'continued fitness to practice' of the doctor, as well as keeping up-to-date with developments in their fields. During the appraisal meeting, doctors are required to discuss their practice with a trained 'appraiser', usually another doctor. In summary, the following are the main points discussed:

1- The GMC 'Good Medical Practice' principles, including knowledge, skills and performance, safety and quality, communication, partnership and teamwork and maintaining trust.
2- Continuous professional development (CPD points).
3- Performance of audits, and quality improvement activities.
4- Analysis of significant events.
5- Record of any complaints and compliments.
6- Feedback from colleagues.
7- Feedback from patients.
8- Review of personal development plan (PDP) of last year and the planned PDP for the following year.
9- Provision of supporting information and evidence for the above.
10- Declaration of health and probity (honesty).

Part Two

Back in Time, Initial Training and Work, from Baghdad to the United Kingdom

CHAPTER 1

Early Surgical Training 1974-1976

My very first two years of training and work as a young surgeon were at the Medical City Teaching Hospital (MCTH) in Baghdad, Iraq, where I joined the surgical team on the third floor at a grade equivalent to the UK senior house officer (SHO) at that time. My three very dear friends, Dr Shawqi Gazala, currently a well-known consultant urologist working in Erbil, Dr Hassan Al-Nakshbandi, again a well-known consultant upper gastro-intestinal (GI) surgeon in Erbil, and Dr Munthir Al-Doori started similar training on the same floor at the MCTH.

The unit was a general surgical one dealing with common elective surgical problems, including mainly upper and lower gastro-intestinal procedures, thyroid surgery as well as breast cancer surgery. Daily management of emergency admissions was part of our commitments as well.

The MCTH in Baghdad was built in the year 1970. It had 11 floors, and included virtually all medical and surgical specialties, both elective and emergency, apart from orthopaedic, transplant and neurosurgery. Oncology services were also provided in a separate hospital.

Excellent and advanced clinical and various support services were available, including radiology, chemical pathology, histopathology and microbiology. An excellent medical library was situated on the ground floor, fully subscribed to most popular journals and with a wealth of textbooks, regularly updated. The MCTH was really representing the 'state of the art' at that time.

Dr Munthir Al-Doori moved subsequently to the second floor, after the first year that he spent with us, to work with Professor Zuhair Al-Bahrani (God bless his soul), one of the greatest surgeons our country had ever known. Professor Al-Bahrani was recognised both nationally and internationally for his contributions to the management of several upper gastro-intestinal diseases, mainly in the field of gastric and small bowel lymphoma. His operative manual dexterity was exemplary.[18]

These two years of training were extremely busy and fully enjoyable, learning various essential surgical skills which all young surgeons are eager to acquire. Besides the technical skills, the MCTH offered the great opportunity of learning and contribution to a very active teaching program for both under and postgraduate students.

In retrospect, and while subsequently working in London and North Wales hospitals between 1976–1980, I always recalled how advanced and equivalent the level and standard of medical services in all its aspects at the MCTH in Baghdad were as compared to UK hospitals.

Shawqi, Hassan and I sat and passed the first part of the FRCS examination, held in Baghdad in 1976. This was a pre-requisite to obtaining the four years' scholarship from the

---

[18] There were several other consultant surgeons at the MCTH whose reputations were again very highly upheld as clinicians, teachers and humanists. Among them were Professors Abdul-Latif Al-Badri, Khalid Naji, Khalid Al-Kassab, Yousef Kattan, Aziz Mahmood Shukri, Tahrir Al-Gailani, Hussain Talib and others.

Ministry of Health in Baghdad, to travel to the UK for further postgraduate training and to successfully pass the final FRCS examination.

Shawqi and I landed in London in June 1976 and applied for the General Medical Council's examination TRAB (temporary registration assessment board). This examination assesses the overseas doctor's knowledge, skills as well as proficiency in the English language. Success at this examination is an essential requirement before being able to apply for any job within UK NHS hospitals. The TRAB exam became subsequently known as the PLAB exam (professional and linguistic assessment board).

Having passed the test, we then applied for posts in different parts of the UK.

We worked at different hospitals from that time onwards, but kept in touch regularly until Shawqi decided to go back to Iraq in 1979, having passed the final FRCS examination, and started working as a consultant urologist at Al-Karama Teaching Hospital in Baghdad.

Photo 5: Medical City Teaching Hospital in Baghdad.

CHAPTER 2

The First Four Years of Working in the UK, 1976–1980

My very first job in London was as an SHO in the A&E department at Edgware General Hospital.

I must admit, as I am sure most if not all doctors from Middle-Eastern countries would also readily admit, that it takes at least few weeks to get used to the new life in a Western country and that is regardless of the nature of work done. Call it cultural shock, which might be the right expression as many others would like to describe it.

In medicine, this time period and adaptation is probably shorter than in other professions due to the nature of teamwork and regular communication with patients and their relatives starting the very first day of working within NHS hospitals.

I enjoyed tremendously the six months I spent in this A&E department particularly, as I quickly felt comfortable and confident with management of patients with various health problems coming through the A&E doors. I'm sure my work and experience in Iraq since graduation in 1970 provided me with the experience which gave me this confidence.

Some interesting health problems, which taught me a lot during this six-month period, come to my mind, two of which particularly stand out in my memory. This was also the time when I realised how vital the issue of 'reflection on my own practice and patients' management' is, and how great its positive impact is on every doctor and health professional throughout their career.

The first patient was a 79-year-old lady who fell while standing, waiting for her bus at the station. She was brought by the ambulance to our department and I was on duty that evening. She was fully conscious but understandably very worried.

I went to see her following initial assessment by the nurse, who informed me that she was fully conscious with no signs of head injury or injuries anywhere else and her mental capacity was normal. Her Glasgow Coma Scale (GCS), was normal (15), and all vital signs normal.[19] I introduced myself to the lady and proceeded to examine her in the presence of the same nurse. She was a very healthy lady, leading a fully independent life, using just inhalers for asthma.

I fully examined her, and then requested few blood tests as well as a chest x-ray an electrocardiogram. Having received the results of the tests an hour or so later, all of which were normal, I went back to her cubicle to reassure and discharge her. I explained to her that her fall was clearly caused by a transient drop in her blood pressure while she was stood up for some time at the bus stop. I was about to leave the cubicle after shaking her hands to go and see another patient, but she looked very worried and stopped me from leaving the cubicle, saying: 'Doctor I'm only 79 years of age now and I need to know what happened and why did I faint. What's going to happen to me in 10 or 15 years' time if I don't know and deal with this problem now?'

---

[19] GCS is used to objectively describe the extent of impaired consciousness in all types of acute medical and trauma patients.

She was right, of course. I felt uneasy with myself, having missed an important aspect in her management, which is to list her for a follow-up visit with a geriatric consultant. I apologised to her and told her to expect an appointment to come back for this follow-up visit.

On reflection, I felt that I learnt a good lesson here. I guess I was initially surprised by her undue concerns in spite of the normal results of her tests and having explained to her the cause of her fall, at her age. Surely, the consultant geriatrician may not consider the need for any further investigations, but that's a decision for them to make, not me. Again, I learnt never to consider age, on its own, as a reason to modify my management plans.

The management of another patient in the same A&E department was again a vital experience and an essential source of learning how proper teamwork management of patients should be.

This was an elderly gentleman brought by the ambulance service, flashing the emergency sign of 'blue lights' to the A&E department late one evening. The history provided by the paramedical staff was of severe chest pain while sat in his house, locally. He was resuscitated in the ambulance while urgently driven to the hospital. The A&E department, as always the case in such situations, is alerted about the forthcoming urgent arrival of a patient.

I was on-call that evening when the patient was admitted to the resuscitation area of the A&E department. He clearly looked very distressed, short of breath and cyanosed, though still on an oxygen mask delivered by the ambulance paramedics. He soon became unresponsive with clear signs of cardiac arrest and required urgent endotracheal intubation;

since the conventional steps of initial resuscitation with chest compressions, mouth-to-mouth breathing and some intravenous medications did not appear to improve the patient's condition. An urgent electrocardiography (ECG) had already showed clear evidence of acute myocardial infarction and very fast irregular heartbeats.

The resuscitation trolley was readily available and I quickly managed to insert an endotracheal tube (an airway device to support breathing) while further resuscitation measures were continued. I was so delighted with myself, and so was the resuscitation team, as our efforts proved successful. The patient showed clear signs of recovery, becoming stable, and was then transferred to the coronary care unit.

However, and to my initial surprise coupled with some element of disappointment, I was criticised the following day during the early morning meeting of the A&E department. These meetings happen every morning, serving several purposes, being educational as well as a handover to the receiving new team.

The meeting is chaired by the A&E consultant with full attendance of junior doctors, nursing staff and the matron of the unit. The point of criticism was that I should have brought the on-call anaesthetist to intubate the patient rather than doing it myself. I tried to explain that my action was based on the urgency of the situation and the fact that there was no anaesthetist immediately available at that moment in time within the resuscitation area. Added to that I also explained that I had gained excellent experience and confidence with endotracheal intubation having worked for more than three months in the coronary care unit at the MCTH in Baghdad.

The points of criticism raised were, first, that tracheal

intubation was essentially an anaesthetic responsibility, and secondly, that if anything did go wrong with my intubation procedure then I would have stood on poor grounds to defend myself if any complications happened or if the patient died.

Well, at the end of the day (as is commonly said in the UK, meaning 'in the final analysis or conclusion of discussions'), I felt the criticisms were well justified. It was also most likely meant to alert all the other junior doctors on the unit about the vital necessity of involving other specialists, when needed, during the management of such patients.

In retrospect, and as a positive sign, I also recall very well that the same A&E consultant offered me an extension to my post in the same department with a promotion to a registrar grade, after having finished my initial contract of six months. I thanked him a lot and apologised that I had to carry on looking for posts in general surgery.

Another patient's case scenario, of an entirely different nature, remains in my memory to this day. This occurred while working in 1977 at the Royal Marsden Hospital (RMH) in London, an internationally known cancer centre. I recall I was breaking bad news to a gentleman around 60 years of age who hads just been diagnosed with advanced cancer of his urinary bladder, already spread to his lungs and bones.

The patient asked me, 'Doctor, how long do you think I am going to live?' I answered that his consultant, who delegated the responsibility to me to break the bad news, reckoned that he would probably live around four to six months, though his final destiny was in God's hands. The patient's expressions hardly changed, which I believe was probably because he already knew that he had advanced cancer. He only replied with an expression of disappointment that he would not be able to attend his daughter's wedding, which was fixed to take place at a certain date in Spain the next year. I had such a great respect to that man, having taught me another great lesson. In spite of the fact that he became aware of his poor prognosis, he remained in control of his emotions, to the extent that his main concern and thoughts at that moment were with his daughter.

In medicine, we quite often feel so humbled by the brave attitude of some of our patients, by the way they face very bad news about their health and manage to cope with sad facts about their prognosis.

The six months of work at the RMH in London exposed me to some of the most major operations on the gastro-intestinal tract and the pancreas. It was a referral cancer centre accepting patients not just from different hospitals in England but also from overseas referred from different countries.

I passed the final FRCS exams in Edinburgh in 1978 and in London in 1979. I moved to the town of Rhyl, North Wales, in mid-1978 to work as a surgical registrar to Mr Owen Daniel, a great and highly respected consultant general surgeon well-known then for the introduction of his new methods in biliary surgery. His operative lists were very much classical of what consultant general surgeons were performing in the UK at that time.

His lists would contain a mixture of procedures on the stomach, colon and breast cancer surgery, kidney stones or prostate removal, gall bladder removal, thyroid surgery as well as lots of hernias. Working with Mr Daniel gave me a lot of confidence in performing major operations.

It was during these four years of my initial training in the UK that, while socially chatting with colleagues from various backgrounds, I felt so proud of answering questions regarding my training in Iraq.

Besides the excellent standard of medical education in Iraq, I reminded my friends of Iraq's great history, its wealth of natural resources and historical sites and monuments stretching from Nineveh in the north to the marshlands in the south. I explained why Iraq's land is historically known as Mesopotamia (or the land between the two rivers: Tigris and Euphrates), where the Garden of Eden is mentioned in books of history and religion. The first civilisations on Earth, the Sumerian and the Babylonian, started in Iraq around 5000 years BC, on the fertile lands of Mesopotamia.

Most of my friends were aware of how rich Iraq is in oil reserves, but hardly anyone knew much about its rich agricultural and fertile soil. The density of date palm trees in the central and southern parts of Iraq is remarkable,

Marshes in the south of Iraq.

producing incredibly numerous varieties of dates, said to be more than a hundred, with very delicious taste. I quoted a saying by someone, that if there are only four palm trees all over the world, then three of them are in Iraq.

I was so delighted when I met again with my dear friend, Hassan Al-Nakshbandi, as he came over to Rhyl to start working with Mr Daniel as his registrar, just at the time when I finished my contract and had to return back to Iraq.

CHAPTER 3

Returning to Baghdad, Iraq, March 1980

I returned to Baghdad on the 1 March 1980. The weather at that time of the year in Iraq is always lovely, a real springtime. I had three brothers, four sisters and my parents. All were in the airport for the reception.

As it happens, returning back to my own family and relatives after a long time of being away, having successfully achieved higher qualification, is an occasion associated with great happiness and pride. It also means daily big meals and invitations which are impossible to refuse or decline, let alone the fact that I was always given the choice of what to order beforehand! In other words, it is impossible to avoid adding few kilogrammes of weight on!

Incidentally, among various personal belongings which I had already shipped from London to Iraq was a slide projector, which I often used during my lectures and presentations later on in Erbil.

I visited then the Ministry of Health in Baghdad and was given the option of working either in Mosul or Erbil. I visited Mosul initially and met with several colleagues, who were previously my classmates when we studied and graduated the same year from its medical college in 1970.

One of them was Dr Kais Al-Wattar, currently a professor in

paediatric surgery in Jordan, and the second was Dr Zakariya Al-Habbal, currently a professor in general surgery in Erbil, Kurdistan. It was a very nice occasion meeting with close colleagues, almost like brothers, and having a chat with them. Both expressed their delight, welcoming me back if I decided to work in Mosul.

I subsequently went to Erbil a few days later to have an idea about the surgical department there. Realising the shortage of surgical staff in Erbil compared to Mosul, I had no difficulty making up my mind. I was soon appointed as a specialist general surgeon, to work in Erbil starting mid-April. Unexpectedly, I had almost seven weeks of free time before starting to work in Erbil, which is about 400 KM to the north of Baghdad.

I went back to Erbil few days later to develop an idea about the whole set up of health services and managed to meet with a few senior colleagues. That was the time when I first met with Dr Abdul Razzak Al-Dabbagh, the most senior surgeon then in Erbil, a fellow of the Royal College of Surgeons of England, a great man and a highly respected surgeon who subsequently became a great colleague and a friend. He gave me a good idea about the situation with surgical services and was very happy that I was soon to join up. Incidentally, Dr Ali Al-Dabbagh, currently the dean of Erbil's medical college, is his son.

I went down the same day, walking inside the city, and visited the great historical Citadel of Erbil.

Erbil, or Arbil (Hawler in Kurdish), is one of the oldest continuously inhabited cities in the world, dating back to 6000 BC. It has been inhabited over the millennia by the Persians, Greeks, Romans, Mongols, Assyrians and the Ottoman Turks.

At the heart of the city rests the 'Erbil Citadel, or Castle', an ancient structure which is estimated to be close to 6000 years old. The Citadel is a fortified settlement on top of an imposing ovoid-shaped tell (a hill created by many generations of people living and rebuilding on the same spot).

Known also in history as Arbela or Arba-ilu (the city of the four kings, or emperors) during the Assyrian Empire, Erbil is currently the capital of Iraqi Kurdistan and its population was around one million at that time.

Several famous tourist sites, some distance outside the city of Erbil, are favourite places for families from Baghdad, Mosul and southern cities to visit during summertime. It's not just the beautiful hilly and mountainous nature and sightseeing which these sites offer, but the significant drop in temperature and humidity which adds to the attraction.

Some of the most famous tourist sites visited are within the following regions and small towns, including: Salahuddin, Sara-rash, Shaqlawa, Gali Ali Beck, Jundian and others.

The other major city in Iraqi Kurdistan is Sulaymaniyah. This surely holds a very special place in my heart, as it is my birthplace. Interestingly, and in spite of the fact that we moved to Mosul when I was only two and a half years of age, memories of a few events in the old house in Sulaymaniyah, with my brother Kais and my parents, are still alive to this day.

Again, the city has been hugely modernised. It is surrounded by beautiful tourist sites including Sarchnar dam and park, Darbandikhan dam, Azmar and Piramagrun mountains and others.

Nowruz, or Newroz, feast, which usually happens on the 21

March every year, is celebrated as marking the first day of spring.[20]

The battle of Gaugamela, also known as the battle of Arbela, which happened near the city of Erbil in the year 331 BC, is one of the most ferocious battles in history.

The advancing army of Alexander the Great fought the much larger army of the Persian king Darius III. In spite of the fact that the Persian king was aware of the advancing army of Alexander, having prepared the grounds to his army's advantage, Alexander emerged victorious due to his army's superior tactics. Alexander moved into Persia and married King Darius's daughter. The king had already been killed during the battle.

Interestingly, Erbil is also very well-known all over Iraq for the quality of its famous delicious kebab meals. I would surely recommend it to any tourist visiting this historical city.

I returned to Baghdad the following day and spent almost every morning for the following six weeks, attending theatre sessions at the MCTH, either assisting or observing different operative procedures done by my previous senior consultant colleagues. I concentrated mainly on urology, all open procedures at that time, having realised the need for such service in Erbil during my recent visit.

---

[20] Newroz literally means 'New Day', celebrated by more than 300 million people around the world. Considered also as the Persian new year, Newroz is considered a very important festival in Kurdish culture, and is a time for entertainment such as games, dancing, family gathering, preparation of special foods and the reading of poetry. Bonfires are lit up, while people will be dancing or jumping over it. These fires symbolise the passing of the dark season, winter, and the arrival of spring, the season of light. The seventeenth century Kurdish poet Ahmad Khani mentions in one of his poems how the people, youth and elderly, leave their houses and gather in the countryside to celebrate Newroz.

PART THREE

Settling in Erbil, Kurdistan, Iraq

CHAPTER 1

Early Years in Erbil

I started working in Erbil mid-April 1980. I was then provided with temporary accommodation within the private wing of the main general hospital. Having two meals a day at the hospital cafeteria, which was adjoined to the doctors' mess, gave me the great opportunity to start learning the basics of the Kurdish language. I always had a small notebook in my white coat pocket, making notes at every opportunity.

Obviously, as is the case with any language, daily and regular communication with people all around you is the best way to learn the basics of the language. In our case, daily contact with patients and their relatives, as well as medical staff, makes it much easier and quicker to learn the essentials of the language necessary for communication.

General surgery in Erbil at that time covered most of what today is subdivided into several subspecialties. The main reason, which still applies today to the practice of general surgery in most cities in Iraq, is the fact that subspecialisation is not affordable due to the small number of qualified general surgeons per population, which makes it impossible to cover the busy service anywhere in the country if the wide field of general surgery was to become fragmented into subspecialties restricting the practice of surgeons only to certain systems and organs.

In the province of Erbil, with a population of probably around a million at that time, we were only six consultant general surgeons holding the fellowship qualification of one of the three UK Royal College of Surgeons (FRCS), as well as one consultant general surgeon with a board qualification from Turkey, (Dr Hassan Hurmuzy) and another consultant with an equivalent qualification in urology (Dr Jawdat Al-Dabbagh), a great gentleman who sadly passed away in 1993 following a short illness. There were also six or seven well-trained general surgeons, some of whom held a diploma certificate in general surgery from Baghdad.

Another issue is the fact that structured training programmes in any of the general surgical subspecialties in the UK (upper gastro-intestinal, lower gastro-intestinal, breast, hepato-biliary-pancreatic, endocrine and emergency surgery) were only started in the mid-1990s.

As a matter of fact, it was only a decade ago or so that strict subspecialisation has taken shape in the UK. Until 2013, I was still performing colorectal surgery, breast and endocrine surgery, common laparoscopic operations and a large volume of day surgical procedures.

Hence, as a consultant general surgeon in Erbil, I was carrying out oesophago-gastric, colorectal, thyroid, breast and biliary-pancreatic surgery. I was also heavily involved in the management of burn patients both in the acute presentation and subsequently in dealing with burn contractures. Basic paediatric surgery was carried out as well, since we never had a qualified paediatric surgeon at that time.

The daily work pattern in hospitals in Erbil, similar to governmental hospitals all over the country, was and still is quite different from the Western style.

The first working day of the week is Saturday. The only national holiday in the week was Friday. Work starts at 8 am and ends at 2 pm. Most of the staff would then have their lunch, followed by a short time of rest and a nap, equivalent to a 'siesta' in Spanish culture. This short time of work interruption was very refreshing, particularly during the very hot summertime when the temperature rises, at midday, to anything between 45–55 centigrade.

However, the reasons behind this short working time in government hospitals, all around the year, were never clear to us since it surely impacted on the training time of both under and postgraduate trainees. Reasons like low salaries, absence of private health insurance companies and reliance on private clinics for better income, as well as staffing levels, were mentioned.

Apart from newly graduated and trainee doctors, almost all other doctors with different specialties would then start their private clinic between 3–4 pm. This would be for variable periods of time depending on how busy the clinic of that specialist was, and usually would continue for several hours.

Outpatient consultation clinics were held regularly within government hospitals during the morning times, free of charge, though attendance of the public to these clinics was minimal compared to their preference to see the specialist in their private clinic during the afternoon. Patients would then pay only the private consultation fees, and most of those patients who needed an operation would then have their surgery at the state hospital, free of charge.

Just to add here, there was no system of taxation on government employees, or any taxation on the income from the private practice of doctors, and I'm not sure if there have been any changes since. The income from the oil revenue was sufficient to cover most of the expenses for health and other services across the whole country.

During the time I worked in Erbil, there were few attempts at implementing some form of centrally organised system of taxation on the private practice of doctors, but that was only short lived and lacked proper standardisation and was strongly rejected by medical professionals. There were several reasons behind that, particularly the low salaries.

To a large extent, the structure of the health service in Iraq hasn't changed very much over the years apart from the proliferation of private hospitals in most cities of the country over the last 15 years. The work pattern in state hospitals remains, as described above, the same across the country.

In Erbil, in the 1980s, there was only one large state general hospital (Al-Jamhouri Hospital, which means the 'Republican Hospital') admitting elective and emergency surgical and medical patients. The A&E department was a separate building but attached to the main hospital. There was a separate state hospital for obstetrics and gynaecology, another one for paediatric medical patients and one for infectious diseases.

In the private sector, there was only one private general hospital, catering mainly for general surgical procedures and two separate day surgery facilities.

Workload

It surely didn't need a long time for any general surgeon to realise how enormous the workload was in general surgery and the huge demand for specialists in different fields to cope with that. I faced so many surgical problems which I had never

41

dealt with previously since I started my training and work in 1974 at the MCTH in Baghdad, and subsequently during the four years of my initial postgraduate training and work in the UK.

Needless to say, the period of time that Iraqi surgeons were granted for postgraduate training and obtaining the fellowship in general surgery from one of the three Royal College of Surgeons in the UK, which is four years, is really very short. As a matter of fact, the whole purpose of the scholarship then was to obtain the FRCS qualification and return back to Iraq, regardless of the quality of surgical training received and the skills acquired.

The fact is that passing the FRCS examination is considered in the UK as the stage when proper surgical training at the grades of registrar, and then senior registrar, starts. This would take a period of time not less than five or six years before the surgeon feels confident to work independently as a consultant surgeon.

I was probably fortunate to have received proper training at the registrar level for two years after passing the final FRCS examination in Edinburgh in 1978. I was then notified by the Ministry of Health, through the Iraqi embassy in London, that I had to return to Iraq, having fulfilled the objective of the scholarship. The financial allowance from the government, which I was receiving regularly during the first two years, was automatically stopped.

I was fully aware that a number of Iraqi surgeons returned home just after having successfully passed the FRCS exam, within a period of less than four years, having received minimal or hardly any training at the registrar level.

My colleagues in general surgery in Erbil were inundated as

well with work before my arrival, and they had no choice but to prioritise what they could do during the available time and theatre space within a single 'state general hospital' then standing in Erbil city.

The following list of very common general surgical problems describes how massive the workload was, though what lacks in this list is the prevalence and incidence of any one of them at any time period due to the lack of proper regional health registry.

1. Acute burns and chronic burn contractures.
2. Goitres (thyroid swellings).
3. Hydatid cyst (parasitic disease) and its complications.
4. Peptic ulcer disease.
5. Gall bladder stones and their complications.
6. Abdominal wall hernias in adults and children.
7. Surgical presentations of tuberculosis.
8. Breast cancer surgery.
9. High incidence of road traffic accidents and assaults.
10. Day surgical cases, the largest in volume compared to others.

The above short list includes just the surgical cases which are performed almost 'every week' under a general anaesthetic.

Surgery for cancers of the oesophagus, stomach and pancreas are much less frequently carried out, for several reasons. These are classified as super-major operations.

Performing such major operations, which were happening once weekly on average, can take more than five or six hours to complete. Unavoidably, the working time would extend well beyond 2 o'clock in the afternoon. I must admit that the whole theatre staff were always supportive in these situations and never complained about staying extra time, being unpaid.[21]

Colonic cancer is known to have much less incidence in the Middle East and Mediterranean countries than in Europe and the USA, though the exact incidence and prevalence remain unknown.

One interesting benign condition of the colon, which is extremely common in Western countries is the so-called 'colonic diverticulosis'. This is a major health problem in Europe and North America, where it is estimated that half of the population older than age 50 years has colonic diverticula. The condition is also encountered, to a lesser extent, in younger age groups.[22]

While working in the UK since 1995, for almost 26 years, the management of patients with symptoms and complications of this condition happens every week, with a significant impact on quality of life for the patients and a huge burden on the NHS financial budget.

Interestingly, while working in Erbil for almost 14 years, I

---

[21] Geographically, cancer of the oesophagus is known to have rather a high incidence along a belt extending from the Honan province in China, across the northern parts of Afghanistan and Iran, north of Iraq and south-east of Turkey. Epidemiological studies have suggested some reasons behind the high incidence of this disease in this part of the world, but the scope and aim of this book does not allow the space to dwell into that.

Unfortunately, the majority of patients with this disease, as well as of the pancreas, are found to be inoperable for several reasons. Advanced age, associated commonly with other medical diseases, and late presentation of the disease with signs of spread prohibit surgical intervention. Any chance of long survival at that stage following surgery, even if technically feasible, is extremely low.

[22] Briefly, colonic diverticulosis is the formation of small air-like pockets or pouches which protrude from the inside lining of the colon outwards.

haven't come across a single patient with this condition. This was not just my own experience, but all my surgical colleagues shared the same. The evidence was solid, as not a single patient with a complication of this condition, occasionally requiring surgical intervention, was ever admitted.

It may well be that, though rare, the condition does exist in the asymptomatic stage and remains undiagnosed due to limited endoscopic facilities at that time as well.

I actually mentioned this fact during more than one of the surgical meetings at the main teaching hospitals in Nottingham, Manchester and Leeds, where I presented my experience in general surgery during the 14 years I worked in Erbil, documented by numerous slides.

I had no difficulty explaining the reasons behind such an obvious geographic difference in the incidence of this condition, which is strongly suggestive of environmental factors as the main, if not the only, cause. In particular, significant variations in dietary habits play a vital role explaining the extreme rarity of colonic diverticulosis in Middle-Eastern and Mediterranean countries. Age span, though higher in Western countries, surely can't explain the remarkable rarity of this condition in the Middle East.

In 1971, Burkitt first described the protective effects of a diet rich in fibre,[23] documenting the low rate of colonic cancer in rural Africa, and suspected that refined carbohydrates in Western countries increased the risk.

The single private general hospital in Erbil surely did help

---

[23] Neil S Painter, Denis P.Burkitt. 'Diverticular Disease of the Colon: A Deficiency Disease of Western Civilization'. British Medical Journal 1971,2,450-454.

to some extent to deal with the surgical load, but the majority of the population, as expected, could not afford to pay the expenses at that time.

As can be predicted, different health problems with demands exceeding capacity faced all other medical and surgical specialties.

Apart from some rich families, the vast majority of patients and their relatives in Erbil, or any other city in Iraqi Kurdistan, would very much prefer to receive their treatment locally than travel south to Baghdad, some 400 KM distant, or northwest to Mosul, 100 KM distant from Erbil. The travelling distance, the expenses incurred, the language barrier and most importantly the fact that patients were always keen to have their relatives close to them until discharged from hospital were vital reasons why the majority of patients were reluctant to leave Erbil.

Management of Burns, a Frustrating Experience

For these reasons, and occasionally due to the urgent nature of the surgical problems, management almost always took place in Erbil. A very important example here is the management of acute burns. There was no burn specialist, plastic surgeon nor well-trained team to care for such a very common and serious accidental injury in Erbil at that time.

I must admit that I could also perceive an atmosphere of relative indifference towards the management of burn patients compared to dealing with all other types of emergency surgical admissions. In a way, the lack of so many facilities desperately needed for the management of burn patients – including a separate burn unit with dedicated well-trained staff, both surgical and nursing – the high incidence of infective complications and the long and protracted course of treatment of major burns were the main reasons for the reluctance of most of the staff to take responsibility managing these patients.

Understandably, long-term complications, most commonly burn-wound contractures causing various deformities and disfigurements, were very commonly observed among those patients who survived this major accidental injury.

Dealing with these acute and sometimes life-threatening major burns took place within the same general surgical wards. Side rooms were available, but the demand far exceeded the capacity.

In other words, it proved a very painstaking effort requiring a significant amount of time to deal with such patients by learning gradually from our own mistakes and experience, hardly supported by a minimal previous exposure to the care of such patients.

As expected, and readily admitted, mistakes during several steps of management of acutely burnt patients were not infrequent, yet constituted a definite learning curve improving the management of successive and subsequent patients.

I heavily relied also on resorting to available books and literature on the management of burns and its complications. Needless to say, it is our patients and their families who suffered most, though their gratitude was always a huge motivation to persevere and improve.

Fortunately, I eventually managed to make available some vital burn creams and ointments (sulfamylon and flamazine), which were the mainstay in preventing burn wound infection. It took quite some time before these two local ointments became available following formally requesting them through different channels.

By early 1982, almost two years after being regularly involved with the management of burn patients, both in the acute and chronic stages, I had become much more confident dealing with this major and very common accident-related health problem in Erbil.

The nursing staff has also become more interested and knowledgeable dealing with these patients, particularly after the two burn wound creams became regularly available.

Having collected a vast number of slides with my own Olympus camera, documenting the management of varieties of burn problems at different stages, I started delivering various presentations to under and postgraduate students as well during regional surgical meetings. I never ignored the fact that I had only limited knowledge when first started dealing with this problem.

It was not until late in the year 1984 when the building of the new much larger hospital (Rizgari Teaching Hospital, previously called Saddam's General Hospital) was completed, opening its doors for all sorts of admissions, giving a breathing space at the old hospital to develop a proper burn unit.

Rizgari Hospital became the centre for most medical and surgical admissions, complicated surgical procedures as well as the main centre for under and postgraduate education. It was provided with advanced up-to-date audio-visual facilities.

Fortunately, this coincided also with the arrival of Dr Mohammad Bajallan, a consultant general surgeon with FRCS qualification from the UK with interest in plastic surgery and management of burns in 1984.

Dr Mohammad Bajallan took over the care of most of these patients. Following that, I kept dealing with fewer numbers of long-term burn complications.

Rizgari Hospital.

In main theatre (from front: Dr Amir Al-Dabbagh, Dr Waleed Khalid, Dr Atiya
Al-Salihy and Dr Suham Al-Babili).

CHAPTER 2

The Fruits of Hard Work and Dedication

The greatest happiness of life is the conviction that we are loved, loved for ourselves, or rather in spite of ourselves.

VICTOR HUGO

As years passed by, I could see my workload getting gradually busier, mainly with patients' care but also with teaching. A relationship with my patients and the society of Erbil, built on proper communication and trust, had developed and I could clearly, and delightfully, perceive it.

It is really difficult to describe the depth of eternal faithfulness and loyalty of the Kurdish people towards doctors who genuinely help them. I sincerely loved my work, feeling always obliged and professionally committed to provide regular service to my patients to the best level I could. As a sign of appreciation, Kurdish patients and their families always expressed their gratitude and generosity by bringing gifts, such as foods, carpets and occasionally a whole live sheep!

Simple gestures of gratitude, like paying the bill for the meal I just had in a restaurant, or taking full responsibility for servicing my car besides providing me with a courtesy car, were frequent occurrences. Their eternal friendliness, respect and genuine love are the most precious gifts.

Culturally, it is impossible and socially rather unacceptable to refuse gifts offered by patients and their families anywhere in Iraq as a sign of their thankfulness towards the service provided by the medical professional. This was particularly the case following successful outcome of operative procedures.

There were several occasions when patients and their relatives insisted on inviting me and some of the staff to a major celebration in their own village, outside Erbil, where they would express their gratitude in front of a large gathering of their people, followed by offering a delicious meal.

One such invitation followed the successful outcome of major surgery for a cancer problem. The patient was the leader of a tribe and the village was some 100 kilometres outside Erbil. Dr Waleed Khalid, Dr Farhad Al-Khayyat (consultant ENT surgeon) and I performed the operation, which took around eight hours to finish. We were escorted, Dr Waleed and I, by the patient's family to the village. The scenic views, with mountains, hills, and green landscapes all around us were breathtaking. The recovered patient and a large number of his tribesmen were waiting for us. We all sat outside on the carpeted grass forming a huge circle. The meal service never ended and was many times more than a three-course meal! Such invitations constituted another opportunity to learn more about the culture and society of rural Erbil.

Great friends like Kaka Jihan, Salar, Haji Khalid, Ibrahim, my previous two secretaries, Mutasim and Farooq, and many others kept in regular touch with me during the last 26 years after I left Erbil. It's no exaggeration to say that I never felt so close to a society and people in my whole life the way I came to feel towards Erbil.

In retrospect, and particularly after my recent visit to Erbil in November 2019, 26 years after my forced departure, I kept recalling with a great sense of delight how such bonds developed.

The provision of humanistic services to the patients and the society in Erbil, as well as maintaining a high standard of clinical and ethical medical education during the difficult circumstances and hard times, which we all experienced during those years of wars and conflicts, constituted a major and unforgettable store of great happy memories of the years of our dedication to our profession and to the society of Erbil.

CHAPTER 3

Expansion of the Surgical Department, 1981–1984

My friend and colleague Dr Hassan Al-Nakshbandi, a well-known consultant general surgeon, returned to Erbil in 1982. Dr Waleed Khalid, a consultant cardiothoracic and vascular surgeon, with a board qualification from Turkey, was also appointed to work in Erbil in 1982.

Prior to coming down to Erbil, Waleed worked for two years at the MCTH in Baghdad for two years with professor Yousuf Al-Naaman. Professor Al-Naaman was one of the pioneers of cardiac surgery in the world, working along with giants like Michael DeBakey, the Lebanese, and Denton Cooley, the American, in Texas.

Another consultant colleague, Dr Nazad Khusraw, with a fellowship qualification from the UK, also joined our staff in 1983. He was a general surgeon with an interest in urology.

Dr Nooraddin Ismail, a general surgeon with board certification from the 'Arabic Board of General Surgery' started to work as a consultant surgeon in Erbil in 1990. He was promoted to the academic position of professor in general surgery in the year 2011.

Hassan and Waleed provided such a great support to the surgical department in Erbil. Hassan's main interests, apart from general surgery, were surgery of the upper GI system, dealing mainly with cancers of the oesophagus and stomach.[24]

With the arrival of Dr Waleed Khalid, thoracotomy (opening the chest for surgery on the lungs and oesophagus) was performed for the very first time in Erbil in 1982. Waleed also performed closed heart surgery for the first time in Erbil.

Performing new and major operations for the first time in Erbil, as was started by Dr Waleed, Hassan and myself, required, besides regular delivery of relevant educational sessions to the surgical team and nurses, the availability of certain facilities and resources to manage any expected or unexpected consequences or complications.

One example was the occurrence of an unavoidable complication in one of my patients, which is the development of pancreatic fistula (the leakage of damaging pancreatic enzymes) following the emergency operation of drainage a pancreatic abscess. There was an absolute need to provide urgent nutrition directly through the patient's veins while stopping all food intake by mouth completely until the leakage stops, which may take several weeks. Such nutritious fluids were never used previously in Erbil's hospitals, and their provision through the formal routes of requesting them from

---

[24] Hassan was granted a professional training and study leave in Tokyo, Japan for six months in 1984, where he learnt the advanced skills in the management and surgical procedures of cancers of the oesophagus and stomach as well as surgery for the condition of bleeding from the oesophagus due to high pressure in the venous blood, which is medically termed 'portal hypertension'.

On his return, he delivered few presentations on these subjects to the surgical department and established his interests in upper gastro-intestinal surgery. He performed, very successfully, these very major operations over the following years.

Baghdad would have taken a long time. To expedite that, I had to drive to Baghdad and meet the MCTH hospital manager, who happened to be a surgeon and a previous colleague of mine. He was very happy to help and provided me with a good supply of the material, which I took back to Erbil. Fortunately, the patient survived.

I am sure that Dr Waleed Khalid, whose chapter comes later in this book, can quote more examples of personal efforts and travelling, given the fact that his field was an entirely new and different one.

Fortunately, and as time went by, we managed to maintain a regular supply of materials and other resources through the formal processes of application to the central suppliers in Baghdad.[25]

Release of the first publication of 'Zanco's Journal for Medical Sciences'

Release of the very first issue of 'Zanco's Journal for Medical Sciences' in 1993 from the medical college in Erbil was a great achievement, both scientific and historical. The credit goes to every member of the editorial board and to all colleagues who contributed to the published articles. Very special gratitude and recognition goes to Miss Ziyan Omer Huwez (scientific researcher and secretary to the journal) for her non-stop dedication and enthusiasm in preparing the manuscripts and supervising the publication and release of this journal.

---

[25] Unfortunately, and because of resource limitations, lack of infrastructure and the costly Iraq–Iran war at that time, open-heart surgery was not possible. He also performed, again for the first time in Erbil, numerous operations on the lungs for various diseases, with excellent results.

This was a great day in my life and in the lives of all the staff, in clinical and basic departments, who worked hard to see it coming to existence some 11 years after the birth of the medical college in Erbil. It was a source of great pride to everyone and, as expected, a great inspiration for scientific progress and research.[26]

It was in this first issue of the journal that I also wrote the 'obituary' on the sad event of the recent departure of our very dear friend and colleague Dr Mohammad Bajallan. He was a great general and plastic surgeon, an artist and a humanist, loved by all colleagues and staff as well as by his patients and the society of Erbil. Mohammad Bajallan took over the full responsibility of constructing the burn unit within the old general teaching hospital during the years 1984 and 1985. His loss was tragic and felt, not just by his family, his colleagues and the hospital staff, but also by the society of Erbil. His achievements are well remembered to this day.

I was very pleased also to learn from Dr Ali Al-Dabbagh, current dean of the medical college, that regular release of the same journal is ongoing to this day.

---

[26] It was also a great achievement that I managed, in collaboration with Dr Waleed Khalid, to publish an article in this very first issue of the journal on a surgical procedure for the management of cancer of the oesophagus.

PART FOUR

Work During the Iraq–Iran war
September 1980 – August 1988

CHAPTER 1

Surgery Near the Front Lines

The unfortunate eight years of war with Iran had its significant impact, as expected, on all aspects of life. As a matter of fact, the provision of important necessities for daily life inside the cities wasn't adversely affected during the first few years of the war, apart from bringing back the coffins of so many soldiers, when possible, following major battles. It was mainly during the last two to three years of the war when air raids and missiles were often launched haphazardly from both warring sides, on the cities, which caused a lot of panic, numerous civilian casualties and deaths.

In medicine, the surgical specialties which were regularly involved with providing services near the war front lines involved mainly general and orthopaedic surgeons.[27] Obviously most other surgical specialties were also involved, but that was more likely to happen at the main military hospitals following initial management at the base hospitals near the war's front lines.

Different hospitals in most major cities in the country produced regular lists on rotational bases of units of surgical staff, which involved mainly general and orthopaedic surgeons with their anaesthetic and nursing staff, to travel to the base hospitals to deal with various and serious war injuries.

---

[27] Vascular and thoracic surgeons were infrequently included in these teams since such departments only existed in major teaching hospitals in Baghdad and Mosul.

Such base hospitals were obviously the nearest, geographically, to the front lines, hence located in cities bordering with Iran like Basra, Kut and Amara in the south and southeast of Iraq, and Sulaymaniyah on the northeast side.

War injuries are so much different from civilian injuries. In fact, it can rightly be considered a surgical specialty of its own. The war was mainly fought by the infantry using rifles and advanced weaponry systems. Most injuries are multiple involving different parts of the body. Prioritising management of the injured soldiers according to the urgency and nature of injuries, requiring life and/or limb-saving, is the first and main principle in war surgery.

The majority of the wounded soldiers were transferred from the front lines in large military coaches to the base hospital. When battles start then the nearest base line hospital is on the alert and the managerial and surgical staff are fully prepared to receive them.

As time went by, it became clear that an arriving coach was always full of the wounded soldiers and higher-ranking military officers, a number of whom unfortunately were already dead on transit or were not survivable. The vast majority of injuries involved the lower limbs, often associated with abdominal or chest injuries. Serious head injuries and major chest and vascular injuries are obviously already fatal on the battleground.

The experience was always sad, frustrating and heartbreaking seeing young soldiers dying in front of our eyes while we are working fast to prioritise who should go first to theatre, who needed insertion of urgent chest drains (to evacuate collected blood in chest injuries) and who needed more pressure on bleeding limb vessels while transferring to theatre.

Every surgeon operating on war injuries has faced situations where the only procedure that could be done is the so-called 'damage control surgery', whereby obviously bleeding vessels, usually within the abdominal cavity, are controlled and dead tissues removed followed by applying pressure with large gauze packs to control further bleeding and close the wound. Once recovered and stabilised, the patient is then immediately transferred to the nearest military hospital for further surgery and management.

As expected, lower limb injuries are extremely common in such wars due to blast and bullet injuries, but mainly caused by treading on mined fields. Amputations were often carried out just at the line of the irreversible damage to save as much length as possible of the limb for further reconstruction at the military hospital.

The liver is the most commonly injured organ in the abdomen, due to its large size and the fact that it is also largely covered by the lower ribs on the right side, making it susceptible to injuries involving the abdomen and the lower part of the right chest. Accordingly, it is often associated with injuries to the surrounding organs. Management of such injuries is beyond the scope of this book and is quite often a challenging surgical problem.

Interestingly, while operating on one of them in the main hospital in Sulaymaniyah, I noticed that the patient started showing signs of recovery from anaesthesia with muscle contractions and movement of the limbs; I turned to the anaesthetist to alert him, only to find him asleep in his chair! He was very tired, having worked non-stop for more than ten hours as his replacement hadn't arrived yet. I had no choice but to wake him up!

In another situation, and while operating on the abdomen with multiple bowel injuries, the whole theatre building was suddenly shaking following the landing of a rocket or a major missile not far away. It felt like an earthquake. Everyone left theatre for shelter, but I had to stay, putting some pressure on bleeding vessels with my trembling hands! Fortunately, no more bombings landed after that.

CHAPTER 2

Compulsory Military Training of all University Staff

In 1986, military training of all male university staff, along with their students, across the country for four months was decided by Saddam Hussein, and was compulsory. These were hard days, to say the least, impacting not just on our work as specialists serving our patients, who desperately needed us, but also on the continuity of the educational responsibilities to our students.

'It is fair to say that there will inevitably be times in the career of a doctor, anywhere in the world, when lack of resources, conflicts, stress and tiredness will stand in the way of best practice.'

So, we were actually trained as soldiers in a military training camp called 'Dibbis', near the city of Kirkuk. Our trainers were just couple of ranks above that of a soldier (nicknamed 'Areef' in Arabic, akin to 'first or second class private'). We all had to wake up at 6 o'clock in the morning and stand in a long queue, along with our students, to get our share of lentil soup and very stiff bread for our breakfast. This was followed by a good run supervised by the military trainer, then some exercises including how to load up bullets into a magazine and shoot a rifle (Kalashnikov). We were shown first how to assemble and join the different parts of the rifle and how to clean its parts with a greased piece of cloth. We were ordered to keep our rifles, unloaded, beside our beds, to be ready for the shooting lesson the following morning, which happened a few times during the whole period of our training.

A couple of interesting incidents during these four months of training come to my mind. The first involved the shooting lesson. The month was July 1986 when the temperature was anything between 50–55 centigrade. My dear colleagues were lying by my side, all flat on our bellies, including Dr Waleed Khalid, Dr Fathil Abbas Abbood and others.

The military trainer, having initially demonstrated to us how to load the bullets into the magazine before fixing it into the rifle's body, was stood up observing us closely to make sure we were doing it fast and accurate. The bullets, some ten or more of them, were spread on the sand beside us close to the rifle's magazine.

So, the whistle was given, and all started loading the bullets. I managed the first two bullets only as I began feeling my fingers burning from the heat of the metal. At that moment I pulled out a piece of Kleenex from the side pocket of my military uniform to hold the next bullet and load it. Well, you may expect how the military trainer reacted to that!

His voice was loud and commanding, shouting: 'Doctor, I reckon you might well be shot and killed by the enemy before finishing the full loading of the magazine this way!' Well, you may guess what happened later, as I developed nasty blisters on my right index finger and thumb!

The second incident happened few days later when Dr Waleed Khalid suddenly developed bleeding from his nose (epistaxis) during training. The military trainer advised some primary aid management, but Dr Fathil and I, as well as Waleed himself, decided that the situation was serious, warranting an urgent transfer to the military hospital in Kirkuk.

Fortunately, we managed to convince the military officer that we should escort him in the ambulance, being doctors, to make sure he remained safe during the transfer. Well, that gave us some breathing time and relief for a couple of days from the extremely hot environment of the military training field.

This compulsory training finished at the end of October or early November, and we returned to Erbil and resumed our regular commitments.

CHAPTER 3

Hours in the Shelter in our Backyard

As is the case with most major wars, particularly when lasting for years as happened with the Iraq–Iran war, the bitter experience and suffering of people can only be genuinely felt by the warring sides. To other countries, East and West, the real picture of what is happening on the ground inside both countries is very much overshadowed by news of the ferocious battles along the borders between the two warring armies.

Civilian injuries were rather common during air raids since targeting military bases and ammunition stores were frequently unsuccessful, and most surgeons would hurry up to the hospitals once the second siren announcing the end of the air raid was heard.

There were times when my wife and I had to wake up our two sons (Wisam was four or five years age and Raed a year younger) from their deep sleep and rush to the underground shelter, dug in our back garden only few weeks earlier, when hearing the horrible sound of the siren signalling an impending air raid from Iran. The loud noise of bombings is almost always heard soon after that, targeted mostly at military bases in Erbil, but not always very successfully! The kids were obviously very scared. My wife and I shared them the same feelings and even worse!

Once the second siren, indicating the end of the air strike, is heard, all general surgeons as well Dr Waleed Khalid would rush to the hospital in their cars as casualties always arrived within a short period of time.

Internal conflicts and armed clashes, mainly between the government's forces and the Peshmerga, were not infrequent during these times, particularly later in the day and at night. There were times when doctors had to leave their private clinics and return home earlier than they would have otherwise, for safety reasons. It was sometimes difficult, if not impossible, to know which sides were involved in clashes inside the city.

I recall a few times, when either Dr Waleed's car or mine required some repairs, that we went to our private clinics and returned home in the same car. On one occasion, returning a bit late was quite scary. Suddenly, and as I was driving, there were the very loud sounds of bullets flying everywhere. We didn't actually know what to do, whether just to park on one side of the road, waiting for the fights to stop, or just to carry on. Instinctively, I just sped up driving. All of a sudden, I felt the car shaking but there was no evidence of any damage to the car.

Fortunately, we reached home shortly after that at Zanco's Village as we lived almost as neighbours. The next morning, as I was parking my car at the hospital's car park, I noticed a male nurse also stepping down from his car and then waving to me with a strange look. He pointed to a hole in the front pillar (the long thin metal piece between the wind shield and my side window). That was where a bullet was seen, having made a hole and stuck!

I guess I couldn't have been luckier than that!

Yet another incident, which fortunately ended peacefully,

happened one late evening during November 1986. This was a situation of forced entry by three armed men into our house at the university housing campus, Zanco's Village, which is located some 4–5 KM outside the main city of Erbil. My wife and I were having supper with our two sons (Wisam was three and Raed two years of age). One of the men said, quietly, 'We know you are Dr Abdul-Amir, a university teacher and a high-ranking member in the Baath Party[28] and we command you to give us your gun and car keys immediately.' I replied that my name is Dr Amir and not Abdul-Amir, and that I was a well-known surgeon in Erbil, not a university teacher, and had no possession of a gun.

I tried to look for some personal identification in my room to confirm what I said, but I was closely observed, and they probably thought I meant to reach for a gun. They were clearly in great hurry and demanded my car keys, after making a quick search around the house. As they left our house, the same man said, 'You will have your car back if you were telling us the truth.' The security guards were late to arrive that evening, after hearing the news of the raid on several houses at Zanco's Village.

A week later, and while working in my private clinic, my secretary was handed a piece of paper by someone who quickly left, after asking him to hand it over to me. On that small piece of paper, the following few words were written: 'We apologise for the mistake. We meant another person not yourself. You can collect your car from Bistana Village.'

By that time, most people in Erbil, not just the university

---

[28] The Baath Party was then the ruling party during the reign of President Saddam Hussein.

staff, had heard about the recent incident in Zanco's Village. I also came to know, a few days after the incident, that a Doctor Abdul-Amir was a university teacher at the science college, and his house was just few blocks away from mine in Zanco's Village. He happened to have the exact car model and colour like mine, a red Volvo 244 DL!

To cut the story short, I was advised that no one could step into 'Bistana's Village' because of major security issues. I received, a month later, a telephone call from the security office in the village of Makhmoor (some 40 KM outside Erbil), advising me that I needed to come down to the village to collect my car.

The message made it clear that I needed to hire a special vehicle to transfer my car back, as it was severely damaged. As I arrived to Makhmoor, I could see my car riddled with bullets everywhere, with the windscreen and side window shattered, as well as two flattened tyres.

The car was repaired fully in Erbil, but I had to sell it few days later.

The war ended in August 1988 when both countries agreed to a ceasefire. Inside Iraq, the feelings were a combination of relief and a sense of victory, mixed with sadness due mainly to the great loss of lives, as well as the expectation of unavoidable economic consequences.

PART FIVE

Educational, Family and Office of the Dean Commitments

CHAPTER 1

Transfer of University from Sulaymaniyah to Erbil in 1982 – Undergraduate Education

In 1982, the University of Salahuddin was transferred from the city of Sulaymaniyah to Erbil. The decision for transfer was made by the central government in Baghdad following the occurrence of incidents due mainly to political conflicts.

The medical college building was just opposite the main state hospital in Erbil and its construction had already started prior to the transfer and was completed shortly after that. For a while, before and after the transfer, the different departments were organised and completed before the start of the academic year in September.

There was a sufficient number of clinicians in Erbil in all relevant departments to cover delivery of the clinical parts of the curriculum. However, the vast majority of the staff and facilities delivering the basic and pre-clinical medical sciences came down from Sulaymaniyah where the university was transferred from.

I transferred my employment, shortly after that, from the Ministry of Health to the Ministry of Higher Education and Scientific Research. I started, with most of my colleagues in different specialties and departments in Erbil, an active teaching program to the medical students. The transfer at that stage included students who have reached their fourth year in the medical curriculum, which consisted of six years to graduation.

Undergraduate medical education, including the curriculum and the teaching program, were on the footsteps of the main medical college in the capital, Baghdad. The latter was established in 1927 through the efforts of many Iraqi doctors such as Sami Shawkat, Hashim Al-Witri, and Saib Shawket, headed by the college's first dean, Sir Harry Sanderson. He established the first medical curriculum in coordination with the Royal College of Surgeons of Edinburgh and set a strategic plan for medical education in Iraq.

The curriculum and the mode of teaching included traditional department or discipline-based lectures, basic science laboratories and clinical-based teaching. The latter was only started during the third year of the six-year curriculum. Some elements of the so-called 'problem-based learning' or PBL-style teaching was first introduced at the medical college in the city of Tikrit, north of Baghdad, in the 1980s, with the aim of replacing teacher-focused style of education to a more integrated, student-based one.

Transfer of the university to Erbil introduced new responsibilities in my duties and commitments as I always loved teaching. The traditional style of undergraduate education, as still existed in most medical schools in Western countries at that time, consisted of delivering lectures to medical students in large classes where all the students of that academic year were in attendance. Clinical teaching on ward rounds involved a group of rather large numbers of students, between 10–20 at any one time. Much lower numbers obviously would be attending theatre sessions and outpatient clinics.

71

All in all, the clinical departments were very well staffed, and our students were extremely eager to learn. Excellent library facilities became available within the following couple of years, again most of which was transferred from the medical library in Sulaymaniyah.

In retrospect, I can happily say that, along with my colleagues from the two ministries (Ministry of Higher Education and Ministry of Health), we managed to develop an excellent tradition, both educationally and professionally, among our students. One might argue that such motivation was expected given the fact that this is a great event in Erbil's history getting this honourable opportunity of having a medical school and the whole university on its grounds. Added to that, the staff of every department, basic, pre-clinical and clinical, were very eager and enthusiastic to deliver the curriculum in the most satisfactory way.

Several well-scheduled training sessions, the so-called 'Training the Trainers Sessions', meant to improve the teaching skills of the medical staff, were held in the science college in Erbil.

This also brings me here to an extremely important point regarding a most vital element in medical education. This is what all medical teachers and clinicians of experience consider to be as crucial as teaching skills and knowledge relevant to this great profession. I'm sure the reader is clearly aware of what I'm hinting at.

Medical professionalism and the building of medical ethics should and must start during the undergraduate years of education. That's what my colleagues and I were very much conscious of, particularly as the whole situation and circumstances in Erbil at that time were very turbulent, given the various ethno-religious backgrounds of the students as well as the staff. Unavoidably, politics always play a part as well, which further complicated the situation.

I guess the deep desire and motivation of the vast majority of the students and the teaching staff to support the educational process to its successful outcome was the main factor which helped to damp down the negative repercussions of various conflicts.

Teaching Medical Ethics in the 1980s, More like a Hidden Curriculum

Previously, most medical schools and colleges did not formally teach ethics. It was thought that most students applying to study medicine had probably already acquired some elements of ethical knowledge and personality.

It was then believed that the student would be able to learn proper medical ethics by observation of the attitudes, behaviour and experience of senior doctors during different encounters, whether in the classroom, hospital wards, meetings or clinics and 'by doing as they did'.

This has changed for many years now in medical schools in many European, North American and other countries. Teaching of medical ethics as a subject during undergraduate years is delivered by various specialists, some clinicians, basic scientists and some ethicists. Assessment of acquisition of ethical principles by the student is carried out during different parts of undergraduate exams.

For a number of reasons, it remains unclear as to how far the teaching of medical ethics, as a separate subject, has been implemented in various medical schools in Iraq.

In this respect I recall how greatly delighted I felt when, during my visit to Erbil in May 2019 attending the surgical congress, I was reminded about my previous lecturing style by a number of my previous medical students, currently specialists, while chatting to them during the intervals between the sessions. Expressing their respect, they reminded me that I always dedicated 10–15 minutes at the end of my lectures inviting questions and comments and then discussing certain aspects on medical ethics.

That's how I started in 1982, when delivering a lecture to a class of around 150 students. With my very first lecture, after welcoming the students and introducing myself, I made it very clear, in a respectful and non-intimidating manner, that I wouldn't allow any student to enter the class once the teaching hour had started.

Besides avoiding distraction of the class and the teacher's attention once the teaching session had started, there was also the vital need for students to learn the principles of punctuality with time at this stage. Needless to say that the lecturer and most, if not all, medical students, will feel more respected by a colleague who doesn't interrupt their attention.

I would always, non-exceptionally, dedicate at least 10–15 minutes, at the end of the one-hour lecture, inviting comments and questions. Quite often there would still be some time to discuss some ethical principles in medicine. Interestingly, when students are offered this opportunity, they feel more confident and pleased to express themselves and enquire about various ethical issues relevant to clinical scenarios they faced during their clinical teaching sessions.

Along with that, I also made it clear that I wouldn't accept male students into ward rounds and clinics if they were not wearing a white shirt and a necktie. My advice to female students was to apply the minimum of cosmetics and for all students to be wearing the white coat. Again, I wouldn't accept a student into these clinical sessions turning up after the session time had started.

I always spent time explaining to students the reasons behind these principles regarding the dress code and punctuality of attendance. There surely were occasions when I knew I was criticised not only by my students but by some of my colleagues for my style and attitude.

I know for sure that most of my students fully respected me for that attitude, having realised and understood how important these issues were as regards to their proper education in classes and clinical sessions. The dress code was vital to our patients and society in Iraq, who always looked at the medical profession with a high esteem and respect.

The majority of people in our society have, in their minds, the image of doctors as select people destined to become doctors from a very early age. The white coat always symbolised the proper appearance of doctors and imparted that feeling and respect. A white shirt and a necktie for male students reflected significantly on the way our society looked at and respected male doctors. I would expect also that most if not all my colleagues would agree with me that excess of cosmetics does not reflect well when female students and doctors are talking to patients and their relatives.

Did my attitude sound intimidating to a percentage of students and colleagues? I'm sure it did. However, the situation at that time was rather exceptional. The society of Erbil was then witnessing the birth of a medical college on its grounds. This society has always had deep respect for medical professionals. Its expectation of the appearance and approach of every doctor, is entirely different from the way the same society would interact with a professional in any other field in life. To the medical professional, this 'first impression' is always upheld with high esteem and respect. There again, the proper teaching of ethics and professional attitude could easily have relaxed, given the long-protracted years of the Iraq–Iran war and various internal conflicts.

I must register here, with all honesty and respect, the great appreciation of our teaching staff and mine to the teaching staff of the university of Sulaymaniyah, who started the educational process of the students prior to the transfer process.

CHAPTER 2

Marriage and Family Growth

I got married in December 1982 and my wife, Dr Afaf, who was then doing her first postgraduate training and work in the city of Ramadi, south of Baghdad, joined me in Erbil. She spent some time as a house officer in surgery and other departments, following which she was appointed at the haematology department in the main general hospital. Within a few weeks, she became very popular within the department. It took only few months for the different hospital clinicians to realise that her reports and diagnostic skills were very reliable.

My first son, Wisam, was born on 25 September 1983. My wife had to have a Caesarean section, performed by Dr Atiya Al-Salihy, a great friend, colleague and a top gynaecologist and obstetrician in Erbil. My wife was discharged home a few days later. We were then living in a rented house in Ainkawa.

The arrival of my first son was a beautiful time in our lives. He was the joy of the whole family as he was growing up. I vividly recall when Wisam was around four months, starting to laugh and recognising slowly the world around him. My wife then asked me, 'How much do you love Wisam?' My almost immediate and spontaneous reply was, 'I love him as much as I love surgery.' It didn't take too long after that for my wife to realise what I meant and how much I really loved him.

Raed, my second son, was born on the 5 November 1984, and Sandra, 'Daddy's daughter', was borne on the 19 January

1989, both; again by Caesarean section, both carried out by Dr Atiya Al-Salihy as well.

In reality, and I readily admit it, my wife was doing most of the great work bringing up our children all these years. I would be there at home mainly late evenings and Fridays, as I was so much absorbed with work and teaching commitments most of the daytime.

Dr Atiya Al-Salihy and her lovely family remain great friends and I visited them twice in the year 2019 when I was in Erbil during my professional leaves. Dr Atiya is still actively practicing as a surgeon.

Proud parents.

CHAPTER 3

Appointment as the Dean of the Medical College, 1989–1993

I was appointed as the dean of the Medical College in Erbil in August 1989. This was a very honourable position which carried with it the great responsibility of supervision and ensuring progress, together with the faculty staff of different departments and clinical colleagues from the Ministry of Health, of the educational process and proper delivery and regular updating of the curriculum.

Without going into the details of this responsibility, which I enjoyed tremendously, also realising the additional load I had to cope with, I surely acknowledge the great enthusiasm and support contributed to the educational process by all my colleagues. This was always the case since the very first years when the medical school started in Erbil in 1982, and the first graduates with MBChB were celebrated in 1984.

The success was great, and the calibre of our graduates was clearly equivalent to graduates from the medical schools in the capital, Baghdad, and in Mosul.

The occasion of formally granting the MBChB certificates to the young graduates was such a time of great honour and delight. The whole ceremony, granting the graduation certificates to students of all different colleges in Erbil, happened always in July in the open atmosphere on the huge space of a large football ground. The results of the graduating exams of students in different colleges of the university are finalised in June, hence the graduation ceremony taking place in July.

In spite of the very hot weather at that time of the year with a temperature soaring up to 45 centigrade or higher, with at least couple of more degrees added up by the very prestigious formal university outfit, the whole occasion was a great joy to all of us and mainly to the young graduates and their families.

The stage where the university president and all the deans were sat was set up in front of all the graduates and their families. As is the case, I believe anywhere else in the world, the dress code of the graduates of each college has a different colour from that of the other colleges.

The time then came for the dean of each college to stand up at the front of the stage and deliver the important message of granting the graduation certificate to his students. The students, stood up, would then reiterate each word and sentence said by their dean. The president of the university, then Dr Khusraw Ghani Shali, would then follow up confirming the granting of the certificate. This was immediately followed up by clapping and hailing from the students and their families.

I would then do the same, calling on the graduates of the medical college to repeat every sentence of the medical oath, a modified version of the famous Hippocratic Oath, in Arabic.

I'm pretty sure that it was in the year 1990, a year after my appointment as the dean of the college, that I recited the oath to the students in Kurdish as well as Arabic.

I surely had some help from a Kurdish colleague the day before to learn exactly each word and sentence of the oath and how to properly pronounce them in Kurdish. My reasonable knowledge of the language at that time did help me to a great deal. I also rehearsed the oath to myself a few times after that.

Reciting the oath in the Kurdish language in front of thousands of students and their families, my colleagues and the whole university staff was greatly received and appreciated, followed by signs of admiration and gratitude which has remained alive in my mind to this day.

In retrospect, and for further satisfaction of my ego, I recall hearing comments and echoes of criticism from different sources the following few days that I should have been more careful before having done what I did at that time.

That was surely one of the greatest, most delightful and memorable days in my life.

As a regular commitment, and following each graduation ceremony during my four years of office as the dean of the college, I used to call the top ten ranking graduates to my office where I would see them individually, again offering my personal congratulations and wondering about their main specialty interest in future.

In spite of the fact that I was somewhat biased towards surgery, I very much wanted to know about their future inspiration. Each student knew very well that I meant to advise, help and guide them in the right direction to achieve their goals in the future.

A significant number of our graduates, over the years, applied subsequently for different specialty training within the country and abroad. I was so glad and proud to meet with a good number of them during my visits to Erbil in May and November 2019. A significant number of them were actively involved with under and postgraduate education in Erbil, having also achieved high academic status.

The graduates who went abroad, mainly to European countries, obtained further postgraduate training in different specialties. I came to know and meet with a good number of them in the UK, most of them having achieved consultant status and been very successful.

As a team, myself proudly being one of them, I always wished to express my sincere gratitude to all my colleagues, to our students and to all the staff involved in the educational process for the very successful outcome and calibre of our graduates.

Those times were not free from stress and turbulence; just the opposite, with the ongoing Iraq–Iran war and various internal conflicts risking all levels of safe delivery of services, besides negatively impacting the regular availability of facilities and resources. The challenges were felt by everyone. Unfortunately, and as expected, several sad incidents did happen. Perseverance didn't drop at all and the process of education carried on.

If I didn't have the occasion to express these feelings of gratitude and admiration previously, then I'm saying it out loud now.

I was also very pleased during my recent visits to Erbil in 2019 when Dr Ali Al-Dabbagh, the dean of the medical college, informed me that the new system of medical education (known as problem-based learning or PBL) had already been implemented within their curriculum, and will hopefully be expanded gradually.

I'm fully aware also that some research has already been carried out on aspects of medical education on both under and postgraduate levels in Iraqi Kurdistan and in Baghdad, hence some grounds have already been set up to make use of the conclusions of these research topics for further action.

Part Six

The First Gulf war and Forced Departure to Iran, January–March 1991

The deadline given to Saddam Hussein and the Iraqi army to retreat from Kuwait was the 16 January 1991. Dr Waleed Khalid and I decided to take our families outside Erbil city a day earlier, for safety. We drove to the small town of Shaklawa, some 50 KM to the northeast of Erbil,[29] where we rented an apartment. Shaklawa is a beautiful town, surrounded by mountains and hills and is a lovely tourist site during summertime. After making sure that both our families have settled, Waleed and I drove back to Erbil.

That night was very uncomfortable in Erbil, as we were expecting, yet again, to hear the horrific sound of the siren any time that day or night. This surely happened after midnight when all electricity was cut off and the city went dark. This was the first day of the war, so-called 'Operation Desert Storm' by the USA and the coalition forces, starting after midnight on the early morning of the 17 January 1991.

Right from the start, it was very clear how hugely different this war was compared to the Iraq–Iran war. Advanced war technology was implemented by the USA, precisely aiming and destroying Iraqi military targets in Kuwait and inside Iraq. The main electricity power stations were destroyed, and the country was living in the dark for a long time. There was no option but to resort to the use of all simple forms of lighting and heating, given the fact that it was still wintertime.

As the first few days passed, Dr Waleed and I felt that it was safe to bring back our families from the town of Shaklawa.

We carried on with our commitments working and teaching, though feeling the pressure of the new stress, as was

---

[29] Shaklawa is a historic city and a hill station in Erbil Governorate, at the bottom of Safeen mountain.

also felt by everyone else. Luckily, hospitals were functioning properly most of the time, having their own electricity generators. There were, however, some gaps in the timely provision of the power on daily bases, the reasons for which we couldn't quite understand, hence resorting to the use of candles and torch lights while performing surgery for emergency cases.

The other very distressing experience was the fast spreading scary information all over the country that chemical warfare might be utilised by both warring sides. This was sometime towards the end of January, as far as I remember. Gas masks were distributed by the military to the public, but it was impossible to know how widely they were available.

The masks were given with some instructions of how to use them. I still recall how uncomfortable I felt trying to fit the mask on my face, let alone the fact that only few people took the news seriously or believed in the benefit of the masks!

Besides covering all our house windows with sticky, thick plastering as a protection in case glass was shattered by the blast effects of bombings, we also resorted to squeezing pieces of wet cloth and towels all around the front and back doors to halt the effect of chemicals, as if to block their diffusion inside the house. The whole experience was so stressful and scary, let alone trying to explain to our children the reasons for doing all that.

Fortunately, none of those horrible nightmares happened.

I always wondered how wars and battles are given titles which give the impression that they all happened in the battlefields. 'Operation Desert Storm' will mistakenly be remembered in history as happening on the desert lands in the south of Iraq and adjacent Kuwait, but doesn't reflect the fact that it was really much more than that. Along with the subsequent bitter sanctions, it affected the life of every family and left deep psychological scars and traumatised the minds of hundreds of thousands of children.

It was some time, if I remember correctly, towards the end of January or early February when air raids were launched on Baghdad by the USA and the allied forces leading to the exodus of tens of thousands of people outside of Baghdad, mainly to the northern cities, for safety.

Our house in Zanco's Village, had three rooms, a decent size reception hall, a sitting room and a large kitchen space. There was only one bathroom with adjoined toilet facility. Every house in Zanco's Village was the same, having also large front and back gardens.

It surely became overcrowded when it accommodated around 15 additional relatives arriving from Baghdad, fleeing on urgent bases. My parents, my older brother, his wife and two children, the younger brother, four sisters, my wife's parents and her brother as well as two cousins were all with us a few days after air raids started on Baghdad.

Well, we all remember those days with a sentiment of nostalgia. The ladies, with my wife as the leader, and some men, were in the kitchen all day long, working on the gas cooker and preparing meals after meals! There was always a queue for the bathroom/toilet. Lots of card games, domino and backgammon were enjoyed. Candles were the only source of light when it started to get dark, around 5 o'clock in the afternoon. Non-stop boiling of buckets of water was ongoing as well for washing, bathing, and cleaning. Luckily, it wasn't summertime!

Despite the limited space of the house accommodating

around 20 or more people, those were sweet times which everyone recalls to this day.

The relatives started to depart gradually back to Baghdad, around four to five weeks later.

It was some time during March when clear signs of uprisings in all the Kurdish cities started to spread. With people concerned for their lives, and with the approach of the Iraqi republican army towards the northern cities, the exodus of more than 1.5 million Kurds and other groups, across the mountainous borders with Iran and Turkey, took place. Dr Waleed and I were alerted by some of our Kurdish friends, in particular by a very dear friend, Kaka Salahuddin Shafi, who advised us to leave Erbil urgently, as well as escorting us outside the city just a day before the main exodus happened.

Luckily, though a risky and surely a dangerous practice, Dr Waleed and I had already stored good-quality unleaded petrol in large containers and kept them in the underground shelters in our back gardens. This was stored for use in the face of emergency and unexpected circumstances to fill up the car petrol tanks and drive away. There was a desperate shortage in the supply of good-quality petrol during those months. At that time petrol was always sold in the black market at very high prices. Unfortunately, most of it was mixed with cheap liquid gas, or probably water, with significant problems and repeated breakdowns during driving.

It was like having a time bomb in one's house. There was a number of serious major burns accidents and deaths caused by the unsafe storage of petrol containers, with massive explosions and fires in several houses in Erbil during those months.

Well, not much could be packed up in a Toyota saloon car

when the whole family is leaving. So, some vital essentials were taken in a hurry, and we headed towards the borders with Iran.

It surely wasn't a pleasant journey at all. Sandra, my daughter, was only two years of age. Wisam was eight and Raed seven years of age. Waleed's three daughters were just a few years more senior in age than my children.

The journey to the Iraqi–Iranian borders took around six to seven hours, as most of the tortuous roads run between and around the slopes of high hills. As we crossed the Iraq–Iran borders, we noticed the presence of numerous displays written in Kurdish and Arabic languages raised to welcome Iraqis entering Iran!

Following close interrogation and checking by the Iranian security officials, we carried on with a longer journey through the northwest of Iran escorted by an Iranian security official ahead of us. We weren't quite sure where we were heading but hoped to end in one of the northern cities where we could settle in a hotel and rest during that stressful time.

To our great disappointment, we ended up in a deserted place outside the city of Khoy, the capital of Khoy county, West Azerbaijan Province in Iran. The place was a camp and its name was 'Zaraan Khoy'. The nearest city was Urmia, some 140 KM to the south. There were only few camps at that time, but we could clearly observe that many more camps were in the process of completion, obviously in preparation to receive many more arrivals.

It was a very hard time we spent in this camp. Every service, as expected, was very basic and primitive. On the following day, the arrival of hundreds of thousands of mostly Kurdish people from the different northern cities in Iraq started to fill up the hundreds of camps already mounted up.

I can't exactly remember now, but it was probably a week or so that we stayed at the camp. As expected, our main frustration was observing the impact of this sudden, very unwelcome and very uncomfortable change in the daily life on our children. That was a really difficult time, more like in a prison, but fortunately we all left it in good health!

Fortunately, and by sheer coincidence, the Iranian camp manager heard Dr Waleed speaking to his family in Turkish some two or three days later while walking around the camp. The manager, like many Iranians in the northwest, also spoke the second language, which is a dialect of the Turkish language, widely spoken in Azerbaijan. He was curious, and following a brief introduction and realising that we were doctors, he mentioned the name of his cousin, a specialist doctor who also studied in Turkey and was working then in Tehran. This was probably one of the happiest lucky times in our lives, as this doctor was a close colleague of Dr Waleed during the times they studied medicine and specialised in Turkey.

What followed next was a phone call, which the manager allowed Dr Waleed to make to his cousin. As often happens in Iraq, so much is the same in surrounding countries, where personal knowledge of influential people might be of great help during times of need. The manager was then instructed by his cousin that our two families must be allowed to leave the camp urgently to the city of Urmia.

We were advised that we leave in an ambulance car, leaving our own cars behind, so as not to attract the attention of all the camp residents. It was also decided that, after settling in Urmia, that Dr Waleed and I should visit a local hospital in Urmia to treat Kurdish patients admitted because of injuries during the same departure from Iraqi Kurdistan. Some of them had also become ill with other diseases.

After settling in a hotel in Urmia for couple of days, Dr Waleed and I returned to Zaraan Khoy and drove our cars back to Urmia.

The rest of the time we spent in the city of Urmia was in a hotel. We actually made a good number of friends and enjoyed a number of invitations as well. Needless to say, Iranian food is delicious, and the people were really nice.

Dr Waleed and I visited the hospital where Kurdish patients were admitted several times. My knowledge of Kurdish was very helpful for communication and reassurance.

Leaving Iran late April/early May 1991, Waleed and his family managed to enter Turkey, as his wife was Turkish. I returned with the family to Erbil three to four weeks later. I must mention here also that my father, God bless his soul, made the trip to Iran couple of weeks before our final return to Erbil to make sure we all were safe.

I resumed my responsibilities as a dean of the college, as well as my work commitments, both educational and clinical, once I arrived back in Erbil and until the forced departure in November 1993.

Family In 1992, In Ebril.

PART SEVEN

Choice of a Career and Medicine

CHAPTER 1

Dedication to Work, as Inspired by My Father

Whenever I sit back, reflecting and trying to remember my childhood years, my father always stands up high as the man who inspired me to develop a sincere, dedicated and deep commitment to any sort of profession I would choose as my future career. He was my first and main role model from whom I learnt what it meant to love and be dedicated to what we do.

As a teacher, he was such a tireless, non-stop-working and dedicated man to his profession. My father was initially appointed as a teacher in a primary school in the city of Sulaymaniyah, north-east of Iraq. I think that was probably in 1942 or 1943. He got married in 1945. Kais, my brother was born in 1946 and I followed him in 1947, both born in Sulaymaniyah. We stayed in Sulaymaniyah until 1949 when my father was transferred to the city of Mosul to carry on with his teaching profession.

Years went by quickly. The arrival of my lovely siblings, all born in Mosul, kept going on and by the year 1967 we were a big family of ten, with four brothers and four sisters. My mother, currently 93 years of age living in Canada, was working non-stop all day long and often busy during the night as well, taking care of a new arrival almost every other year.

As is the case with most similar large families in Iraq, we lived all together in the same house. My father was teaching almost all day long. He always cycled to the government school in the early morning, starting at 8 o'clock, and is back around 2 o'clock in the early afternoon for lunch. After a short rest, he would then be cycling again to the main prison in Mosul where he was involved in teaching prisoners.

He would then be back around 7 or 8 o'clock in the evening for dinner. There would almost always be some additional, private teaching session to a student for an hour or so. He worked almost 12 hours every day. Quite often, he would also deliver a private teaching session on Friday, the only national holiday of the week. He had to work so hard in order to satisfy the needs of his large family.

In retrospect, the striking feature and character of my father, which I still vividly recall, was his great love and dedication to his teaching profession. He taught mainly mathematics but would often give teaching sessions in science as well, mainly physics.

In spite of the fact that he was working six days a week, and occasionally on Friday as well to a private student, he always looked happy when back from any of these teaching commitments. He was a very well-known and respected teacher of mathematics and physics in our community and was promoted to teach the subjects to students at higher levels than primary school, graded as intermediary and high-school students.

Everyone gets upset and nervous for a number of reasons in life, particularly when feeling so responsible being the only breadwinner for a family of ten, but my father was never bored or tired or fed up with teaching. He taught all of his children mathematics and physics during their times in school.

It's great to have a role model, or models, during our lives and different stages of education. They sure inspire us and make our choices in life easier and more successful. My father was my best and top role model.

My father retired in 1983, at the age of 63, yet he carried on teaching privately in Baghdad and only stopped about ten years later, for health reasons.

And so that was how my father succeeded, unavoidably, in building a strong feeling inside me and inside my brothers and sisters of great love and respect for teaching and for dedication to work.

My mother, on the other hand, like so many mothers in our society, provided all her children with her unconditional love and care. Every new birth was, to my mother, just like her first child. There are no words which can express how happy we all were despite the crowded house with non-stop demands from each one of the growing eight children.

My father inspired me greatly, year after year, towards my choice to study medicine. His devotion, enthusiasm and non-stop dedication to his teaching profession made my decision much easier without any conflict in my mind regarding the choice for any other profession.

I guess at that time, and surely today, that most families in our society would love to see at least one of their grown-up children be accepted to study medicine, as it is also a reason to boast at family gatherings.

I surely would add here that most graduates from high school were keen to study medicine for humanistic reasons as well, realising its great positive impact on their lives and the lives of the patients they would treat. That surely was my main motivation to study medicine.

Professionally, three of us became doctors (Taghrid, the youngest sister, a dentist), my senior brother Kais and younger sister Zuvart became engineers.

Insaf, the younger sister, followed the path of our father and became a very successful teacher of physics and mathematics to high-school students. The youngest brother, Nashwan, studied environmental sciences.

Ilham, the second girl in our family, graduated as an accountant, but eventually became the main carer of my mother over the last 12 years or so. She has been and still is the 24-hour carer of my 93-year-old mother, who suffers from several health problems. Both Insaf and Taghrid provide help as well but the main responsibility has been on Ilham.

Despite the repeated advice from the family physician to move my mother to a nursing home on permanent basis, my sisters remain very reluctant to do so, having realised the huge negative psychological impact on our mother after having spent a couple of days in a nursing home.

In our culture in Iraq, it is a sacred responsibility of the offspring to take care of the elderly in the family. Nursing and residential homes for the elderly are available but very infrequently considered by families, apart, occasionally, for care at the end stages of life.

Unfortunately, our family lost three members (may God bless their souls); the first was Salam, the young surgeon who was 27 years of age and was killed when returning back from Basra in 1983, in a car accident with an army vehicle. His memory remains vibrant in our minds to this day as he was a brilliant young surgeon, full of life, and a great loving gentleman. My second brother, Nashwan, the youngest in our family, was 39 years of age when he was killed by a stray bullet in 2007 While rushing back home during fierce fighting between two sides in Baghdad.

My father was hit by a speeding car in 1997, while I was working at Huddersfield hospital, West Yorkshire. He died the same day, shortly after being taken to the hospital. I was told that the driver came himself to our house in Baghdad the following day, deeply apologising and offering compensation. My sister Zuvart, a devoted Christian currently living in Ainkawa in Erbil, accepted the apologies and declined any compensation. I wasn't sure whether the driver was convicted at all by law or whether he was let free just because the family didn't make any formal complaint!

Unfortunately, such accidents were not uncommon, particularly during those years, and there were many families who suffered losses because of car accidents, internal conflicts and other incidents.

My brother Kais studied electrical engineering in Leeds, England, from 1962 to 1968. I was initially very much tempted, by my brother, to apply for a scholarship to study architectural engineering in England when I graduated from high school in Mosul in 1963.

Besides the temptation to join my brother, the other reason was my great interest in sketching and drawing, which I developed during my early school years. However, I dropped that idea shortly after when I realised how deeply I felt towards medicine.

In retrospect, I soon found out how useful that skill of drawing was while communicating with patients and relatives in Iraq and the UK, making sketches of the part of the body while explaining their disease condition and how to manage it. It was also quite interesting when I found out, while working in the UK, that the Royal College of Surgeons of England was running courses in London for surgeons to learn sketching and drawing while communicating with patients.

CHAPTER 2

Career Aspiration and Inspiration

As has obviously been experienced worldwide, advances in all aspects of technology and sciences during the second half of the twentieth century have led to significant changes in the way we work and live our daily lives. The choices of future careers for graduates of secondary schools, particularly in Western countries, have significantly increased.

Certainly, equivalent graduates in the Middle East have also faced choices for studies in new fields, offering more chances and opportunities for career choices.

Understandably, medicine will remain a highly desirable profession in virtually every society in the world. Besides the principal humanistic motivation to treat the sick, alleviate pain and repair injuries, there are other obvious reasons and advantages associated with this career. These include the social prestige, job and financial security, self-satisfaction levels and the currently available numerous choices for specialty selection within medicine.

The young graduate from high school would select their future career choice depending on several factors. Apart from the effect of the level of marks achieved at graduation, which by far remains the most important factor for Iraqi graduates, there are other elements which impact on the decision for a particular career.

A cross-sectional survey was carried out by Nesif Al-Hemiary et al in 2017,[30] on first-year medical students admitted on the academic year 2015–2016 to Baghdad College of Medicine, University of Baghdad. The students were invited to complete a structured questionnaire, administered through the college electronic education portal.

The purpose of the questionnaire was to try to find out the reasons behind the students' application to study medicine. The questionnaire included data about age, sex and the mean of grades in the last year of secondary school. There were nine questions in total that explored the student's reasons for choosing to study medicine. The response rate was 50% (152 students).

The main reason quoted, at 61%, was 'personal choice without family pressure'. This included 'humanitarian reasons, childhood dreams, positive community appraisal of doctors, and ready availability of work for doctors.'

Parents vision and choice influenced the students' decision to apply to medical school at 38%. This surely reflects the good status of medical profession in Iraqi communities, but family's wishes might sometimes contradict the student's wish by directing and persuading them to apply to study a field which was not their first choice, and job dissatisfaction will be an unavoidable consequence.

Achieving very high marks at secondary school graduation was quoted as influencing the decision at 28%.

In Iraq, there is a perceived expectation by society that achievers of top marks at secondary school graduation ought to apply to study medicine, rather than other professions.

[30] Nesif Al-Hemiary et al. 'Why people apply to medical school in Iraq?' J Med Educ Curric Dev. 2017 Jan-Dec; 4: 2382120517726997.

Dentistry, engineering, sciences and law and other studies would follow, in a more or less descending order of preference, depending mainly on the level of marks achieved. In other words, a student with top marks whose main interest is to study physics, for example, would feel reluctant to do that because of family and social pressure and expectation.

The questionnaire also highlighted that 73.6% of the students made some inquiry about medical school before making their choice, and the people asked were most frequently a medical student or a doctor. However, there was no available help or advice to the students regarding their choice offered by some form of career guidance in the high school prior to application, or by a certain department in the medical school.

The response rate of the survey was 50%, which might obviously affect the results one way or the other. The authors of the study acknowledge this fact and rightly suggest that further study to have a mandatory survey across the student population should be conducted.

Again, there is no mention of the benefits of exposure of the students to the hospital environment, to witness the teamwork nature of medicine on the wards and clinics prior to their application.

This so-called 'work experience' in the UK, for a minimum period of one week, is considered an important element supporting a student's portfolio when applying to medical schools.

Quite often, students aspiring to study medicine in a particular medical school in the UK and other countries would also visit that school beforehand, having already made an appointment to have a chat with the undergraduate tutor for further exploration and advice.

Career guidance never existed previously during high-school education in Iraq and I'm doubtful that it exists today. This obviously leaves the graduates to make their decision regarding future career choice built on factors already mentioned. Naturally, parental influence also plays a part here, particularly if one or both were doctors. Role models, apart from parents, are not often seen as an element influencing career choice.

On their own, the short times dedicated to face-to-face interviews of such applicants to medical colleges in Iraq, as is still happening today prior to final acceptance, are very unlikely to give a good impression about the genuine motivation of the candidate to study medicine.

In effect, given all the factors mentioned above, it should not be surprising that a percentage of very intelligent high-school graduates would have their main interests in other future careers diverted to medicine.

I'm sure that some of my colleagues in Iraq would certainly agree with me, knowing some bright students either in their own family or among their relatives or friends whose career aspirations and application to study a particular field in the university did not materialise, sometimes due to minor differences in the grades achieved at graduation from high school.

Obviously, there are more opportunities to students in Western countries to apply to study medicine or other sciences in another country if their marks did not qualify them to compete for a place in that field in their own country.

I can quote two living examples here: one is in my own family and the other of a very dear friend of mine.

Among my three children, Wisam's interests were in

psychology and he graduated with honours from the University of Western Ontario in London, Canada and subsequently obtained two master's degrees, the first in developmental psychology and the second in the field of 'couples and family therapy'. He is currently applying for PhD study in clinical or developmental psychology.

Raed, my second son, was always interested in studying medicine from a much younger age. He did that at the University of Ottawa. He subsequently specialised in the fields of medical gastro-enterology and hepatology.

Sandra, my daughter, graduated from high school in 2007 with high grades and applied to study civil engineering at McMaster University in Hamilton, Canada. This was for four years, 2007–2011. At a much younger age she spontaneously developed an interest in sketching and drawing. Due to this passion, she initially wanted to apply to an architecture program. However, the program required a highly involved portfolio, which she did not have and was not made aware of in school; hence she applied to study civil engineering. She wasn't interested in studying medicine. Initially, and particularly during her first year at the university, she wasn't happy or sure that she had made the right choice for her future career. However, she carried on with her studies and graduated in 2011 with honours. Following that, she worked initially as a civil engineer for two and a half years. At that stage, and during one of my visits to the family in Canada, Sandra told me that she was interested in studying 'fashion design' in Toronto, a passion she always felt for. The course was for 18 months. I fully supported her, even though it meant an interruption of her engineering job for that period of time. She excelled during that course and won several awards and competitions, besides the certificate. After she graduated, she returned to work as a civil engineer as the income for a fashion design assistant proved to be much lower than her current occupation. After working for three years as a consultant engineer, she was hired as a development coordinator in the municipality where she was, then promoted to the position of project manager in June 2019. Increasingly, and at the same time, she became interested in graphic design (GD), a topic she learnt and excelled in during her fashion design years. She began this hobby in 2017, but only for a short time. However, towards the end of 2019, her interest in GD grew rapidly. She started her side business by designing and creating wedding stationery for brides and grooms.

She carried on with her work as a project manager and started 'working from home' during the Covid 19 pandemic. This gave her additional time to improve her skills in GD. She opened an online shop selling digital art, while offering custom work to small businesses, designing logos and business cards. As she was finding success with the methods and strategies she was using to promote her GD services, she discovered her true passion, which was to teach others what she has learnt. In October 2020, she started a new YouTube channel under the business name, Sandra Di. She teaches others how to start a GD side business from home and how to sell digital products online. Her dream is to create a digital course that walks people through the entire process of discovering their niche in GD, how to create digital products, and how to find clients on a consistent basis. Although she still loves fashion design and gets requests from people to create accessories for them, she has had no time to devote to creating physical products. Digital products are her passion and she intends to grow her side business, probably into a full-time job in the near future.

In conclusion, the reader may wonder why I have dedicated so much space writing about Sandra. Believe me, it's not just because she is my daughter! The fact is that she is now so much happier, having realised that her dream career has finally materialised.

The question, which probably can never be answered correctly, is how many young people eventually felt happy that they have made the right choice regarding their career? How much of that decision was built on their own informed consent and personal interest rather than being influenced by one or more of many other factors, including family, social, cultural, economic, and availability of resources, to name but some of them? Not to forget, of course, that the opportunity to change a career is not all that easy in many countries.

The other experience was with a very close friend. As children we lived as next-door neighbours in Mosul, Iraq for several years during the 1950s. In fact we were just like one family. The two brothers, Hilal and Raik, were of almost similar age to me and my brother Kais. As time passed by, it just happened that I met Hilal again in 1963 when we were both applying to study medicine at Mosul University.

Raik, the younger brother by two years, was still at school at that time. His parents, though, were eager for him to pursue university education in medicine, just like his brother, in two years' time. However, he developed a fever during the final baccalaureate examination and missed sitting the test on one of the subjects. He therefore re-sat the test later during the second term and attained his expected full mark. However, this just meant that he couldn't apply to study medicine due to strict university regulations.

Raik's own interest, as he always told me years earlier, was to study physics, hence was quite happy applying to the science college in Mosul. Raik subsequently excelled at graduation and was sent on a scholarship leave in 1970 to England in order to gain PhD qualification in physics.

He found research in England most stimulating and was awarded a merited doctorate in nuclear physics for developing two new methods. He subsequently held academic and research posts at several academic and research institutions, and gained professorship in nuclear physics at the University of Oxford. Here he was driven by curiosity to fulfil aspirations he had held since he was at Mosul by working at Oxford across diverse disciplines and becoming an international authority on the interfacing between sciences, archaeology, art, history and conservation.

In conclusion, Raik would have definitely been accepted into the medical college in Mosul had he not missed one of the baccalaureate tests due to unforeseen illness. He would probably have found it difficult to object to his parents' sincere wish that he apply to medicine just like his brother, in spite of the fact that his main interest was to study physics. I would advise the interested reader to Google the name 'Raik Jarjis' to understand how great his achievements have been. He remains very actively involved in research and supervising PhD students in the fields of his interest.

PART EIGHT

Lessons Learnt the Hard Way – Dedicated Mainly to Medical Students and Doctors in Training

CHAPTER 1

Post-operative Complications – All Surgeons, all Grades, are bound to face them

In his book *Complications*,[31] Atul Gawande wrote: 'There are surgeons who will see faults and mistakes in everyone else except in themselves. They have no questions and no fear about their own abilities. As a result, they learn nothing from their own mistakes and nothing of their limitations. One surgeon said: "If you are not a little afraid when you operate, he said, you are bound to do a patient, one day, a great disservice."'

I was initially reluctant to include a chapter on 'post-operative complications' in this book, mainly because it may appear as beyond the scope and relevance of the intended messages of the book. However, reflecting on my own surgical experience and practice, spanning now for more than 47 years (since 1974), I thought there are some useful points I could add; mainly addressed to my junior surgical colleagues, particularly during their training years, as well as medical students in their clinical years.

Throughout these years I lived and worked in entirely two different cultures, Iraq and the United Kingdom.

Apart from socio-cultural differences between the two

---

[31] Atul Gawande. Complications, *A Surgeon's Notes on an Imperfect Science.*

countries, the basics of the principles and practice of medicine are surely expected to be the same. Unfortunately, various conflicts, crises and wars are bound to affect all aspects of different services to various degrees. This was the situation for more than two decades in Iraq. The negative impact is on the regular availability of resources, facilities and trained personnel as well as on safety.

My first admission here is that, like all surgeons performing different and major operations, I faced and dealt with a number of my own post-operative complications, whether in Iraq or the UK.

The fact is that I learnt a lot from my own mistakes and from others' mistakes as well. I admitted to that during my learning curve dealing with acute and complicated burn patients in Erbil.

Post-operative complications will always happen, anywhere in the world, and in the best and most advanced centres and hospitals. Quite often they are not avoidable, particularly when operating in emergency situations and on patients with a background of certain medical illnesses. Again, very major operations as for certain cancers, cardiovascular procedures and others are associated with a certain percentage of expected complications.

However, some other complications are related, in a small or large extent, to other factors including what is termed 'latent or system factors' and lack of healthy 'team-work environment' and proper communication. Surely, some are related to individual factors including certain technical aspects during surgery or inexperience of the surgeon.

In this respect, one of the GMC principles of 'Good Medical Practice' stresses the point that every doctor should work within the boundaries of their knowledge and training and not perform a procedure or part of a procedure they are not trained to do independently.

There is probably no surgical procedure, however minor, which is not followed by certain consequences or minor side effects. A not uncommon situation is when a clean post-operative wound might eventually become thick in a certain percentage of patients (hypertrophic scar, or the so-called keloid), which might be associated with some undesirable local symptoms.

Again, the surgical community is well aware of a small percentage of patients who, unavoidably, develop internal abdominal adhesions several years following the straight-forward, usually simple operation to remove an acutely inflamed appendix. A very small percentage of these patients, probably around 1% might even require major surgery (Isaksson K et al),[32] because of development of bowel obstruction due to the adhesions.

I do recall some words from a consultant surgeon, Professor Gazet, at St George's hospital in London in 1976, when Dr Shawqi and I did a period of clinical attachment under his supervision and before we actually started working.

Professor Gazet was reviewing one of his patients in the outpatient clinic after having operated on her recently. She was experiencing some difficulty in swallowing following surgery for a benign condition of her oesophagus, which is known by the medical term 'hiatus hernia'. This was a known, though not very common, complication after that operation. He reassured

---

[32] Karolin Isaksson et al. 'Long-term follow up for adhesive small bowel obstruction after open versus laparoscopic surgery for suspected appendicitis'. Ann. Surg. 2014 Jun;259(6): 1173–7.

her and explained that she would need some simple non-operative procedure to improve her swallowing.

After the patient left the clinic, Professor Gazet did ask us what we thought about the complication. We weren't quite sure how to answer him, apart from knowing the reasons behind that. He realised that we were reluctant to comment any further. He smiled and said, 'Remember, if any surgeon tells you that he or she doesn't have any complication after their operations or that none of their patients died after surgery, then they are either lying or not doing any major surgery.'

I was once listening to a presentation by an Indian professor of surgery, who readily admitted that he had learnt so much from his own mistakes, adding, with a sense of humour, that he was thinking of making more mistakes in order to learn more!

Having said that, it has become very clear in medicine over the last few decades that the real causes of complications, errors and mistakes are multifactorial. There are what we call individual (overt) and system (latent) factors, contributing to the occurrence of errors.

As Moorman wrote in 2007 (*Communication, teams and medical mistakes*),[33] latent conditions for error exist in any system, and teams must be vigilant to identify and eliminate them. When medical errors occur, caregivers (doctors and nurses) often blame themselves, and overlook the complex series of potential contributors. When we as surgeons fail in our goals for patients, we feel accountable and responsible.

---

[33] D W Moorman. 'Communication, teams, and medical mistakes'. Ann. Surg. 2007, Feb,245(2):173–5.

More than four decades ago, Charles Bosk summarised the perceived surgical responsibility for poor patient results, particularly after surgery.[34] 'Deaths and complications present different questions to different specialists. When the patient of a physician (non-surgeon/internist) dies, the natural question his colleagues ask is, "what happened?" But, when the patient of a surgeon dies his colleagues ask, "what did you do?"'

By the nature of the craft, it is much harder for a surgeon to claim or prove that the poor outcome of surgery is not entirely due to their hands, when compared to poor outcomes of patients under medical colleagues.

Very major surgery, e.g. pancreatic and oesophageal cancer surgery, is always associated with a well-known percentage of post-operative complications, even in the best cancer centres in the world.[35]

The message I wish to convey here is one of active communication with our patients and their families a few times ahead of any operative procedure, no matter how simple it may appear to be.

---

[34] CL Bosk. *Forgive and remember: Managing medical failure.* University of Chicago Press, 2003.

[35] Admittedly, I had my share of post-operative complications, which occurred mainly following surgery for cancers of the oesophagus and pancreas. Happily, I managed to deal with complications following my pancreatic cancer operations successfully, but unfortunately, a few patients didn't survive following surgery for cancer of the oesophagus. For proper documentation, Dr Waleed and I worked together in the field of cancer of the oesophagus and published two papers in this field. Dr Hassan Al-Nakshbandi was the first in Erbil to perform a different procedure on cancer of the oesophagus.

CHAPTER 2

Communication, Communication and Communication

'Treat your patients as you want to be treated yourself.'

ORLO CLARK, AMERICAN PHYSICIAN

The main point I want to stress here again is the so-called doctor–patient relationship, teamwork and communication. The time spent in the clinic or on ward rounds with each individual patient is a very precious time when utilised properly. Patient's understanding about their health condition, when explained in simple terms, is always rewarded by satisfaction of patients and their relatives, and by a much lower element of dissatisfaction when certain complications develop.

I never accepted the suggestion that a certain percentage of patients, in my society in Erbil, were not interested in knowing what sort of disease they have developed and what sort of treatment or surgery they needed. I have no study of my own to prove that, but just firm confidence about this vital aspect of management, constantly and regularly experienced during my very busy practice and work as a consultant general surgeon in Erbil for almost 14 years.

Surely there are situations where attempts at explanation,

for example to an elderly patient with various health problems, may not always achieve its objectives. But then, there are always the relatives, particularly in our culture, where at least one first degree relative accompanies the patient.

In any society or culture, most adult patients wait eagerly in a clinic or in their hospital bed to be seen by the doctor, with an element of anxiety. It is our duty, ethical and professional, to try and alleviate that and explain the problem in simple terms which they or their relatives understand. This approach, to my firm knowledge, helped me greatly in dealing with post-operative complications, having already built a strong understanding and communication with patients and their relatives.

On the Day of Surgery

We all are aware how vital it is to visit and reassure our patients on the day of their surgery. Again, I'm sure that every surgeon has their own way of doing that. My own way is first to visit the patient on the surgical ward before being transferred to theatre to alleviate their anxiety and re-explain the procedure in simple terms which they would reasonably understand. I will be ready to answer their questions at that time as well.

I will subsequently see the patient within the reception area of the theatre complex before being transferred to the anaesthetic room. This is an important stage as most patients are being operated on for the first time, some of whom are expected to be very anxious in this new environment. I will then see them briefly in the recovery area, after surgery, and before being returned to the ward.

The fourth time I would see the patient is after I have finished my theatre list and would then go up to the ward to see everyone I have operated on, unless it was a day surgical procedure when some of them might have already gone home.

I have learnt not to miss any of these four steps, after having paid a price for bypassing any of them!

Besides the element of satisfaction of my patients and their relatives seeing me at various times during the day of surgery, it's also vital to exclude any early post-operative complication, which can be managed easier at that time.

The advances in technology have been unprecedented during the last three to four decades with incredible advantages to our patients. Earlier diagnoses, advances in interventional procedures as carried out mainly by skilled radiologists obviating the need for operative procedures in many situations and identification of pre-symptomatic cancers and other diseases are obvious great advantages. However, we ought to be careful utilising this technology lest the pendulum swings too far one side or the other.

There are some important drawbacks associated with such technological advances. Unavoidably there is bound to be an element of abuse and unjustified excessive demands on the use of these technologies, particularly diagnostic radiology, hence leading to less concentration on clinical assessment of the patient by doctors. Excessive requests and reliance on these investigations, mainly radiological and laboratory, is widely practiced in the West and is called 'defensive medicine'.

Obviously, and overall, technology has been fantastic, and the progress has been far beyond expectation.

Another aspect of communication leading to significant

improvement in health services and outcome is the so-called 'teamwork'. My medical readers are well aware of the significant reduction in mistakes, complications and even in mortality following the implementation of the WHO surgical safety checklist globally over the last two decades in operative theatres, endoscopy units and other clinical scenarios.

Healthy and proper teamwork and communication is well-known to improve service and reduce adverse incidents in many fields in life. The well-known significant reduction in airline disasters in the 1970s followed the implementation of strict safety checklists and proper teamwork in the aviation industry.

Outcome of one personal example of teamwork and effective communication

I can quote my own example of teamwork and effective communication while working in Trafford Hospital in England since the year 2001. The operation of removing the gallbladder by the keyhole method (laparoscopic chole-cystectomy) is an extremely common one. Until the year 2006, patients were staying in hospital for at least one day after surgery.

Having read several articles on this procedure, I started implementing the approach of same-day discharge of most patients. This required the following steps, beforehand: 1 – explaining to the patient and their relatives the safety of same-day discharge and providing them with an information leaflet about the procedure, and a contact number to the hospital if they experienced any problems after discharge. They must have at least one person who should stay with them a minimum of 24 hours. 2 – along with the anaesthetists, we explained to the recovery staff and ward nurses certain aspects of care to enhance their discharge. 3 – I visited several practices explaining to groups of general practitioners the safety of this new approach and requesting that they also reassure patients when they visit them prior to surgery; and 4 – The work was carried out within a purpose-built day surgery unit adjacent to, but separate from, the main hospital, with a car parking space.

The benefits of this approach, as my colleagues are aware in the UK, is multiple. Patient satisfaction was recorded and was very high. Lots of benefits to the hospital are gained.

In 2009, Trafford General Hospital was quoted by a special NHS committee as the top in the north-west of England in achieving the highest percentage of same-day discharge following this operation. My own results reached around 80% and, pleasantly, earned me the award of best clinician in the year 2013.

The essence of quoting this success is obviously high-lighting how proper teamwork can achieve it. The operative procedure itself is ranked as much less complicated that many others, hence it was the 'teamwork' of several actors that made it succeed.

Reflection and recording of errors and mistakes

Errors and mistakes are very common events during all different aspects of healthcare, mainly in hospitals, but also in other health facilities like primary care and other institutions. There is a separate system for recoding these incidents by the involved health staff. Their analysis again provides a great opportunity to learn many lessons, with benefits mainly to subsequent patients and to the health institute.

'All surgeons are human. However careful, however experienced, and however conscientious a surgeon is, errors will occasionally occur compromising patient safety.' This has been expressed very clearly by Sir Liam Donaldson, a previous chief medical officer for England in 2004 when he said: 'To err is human ... to cover up is unforgivable ... to fail to learn is inexcusable'

Regular and almost daily post-operative follow up of our inpatients by us as specialists who performed the surgical procedure, including on Fridays sometimes, just enforces the trust and confidence already built up.

Under no circumstances did I mean any lack of confidence or was undermining the assessment of my junior doctors on the wards when I was visiting my patients during late evenings or on Fridays. On the contrary, my visits were as much of an educational purpose to the on-duty junior doctors and nurses as for reassurance to my patients. It was also vital to make sure that every patient was stable.

What I wish to highlight here also is that the good level of care we provide to our patients should be the same whether a patient was the first or the last one we see in a busy clinic or a long ward round. Again, we should be careful not to bypass or just give a brief look at a very ill or terminally ill patient in a side room or on the general ward. Listening to such patients and their relatives, by their bedside, providing adequate pain relief, comfort and dignity, is always greatly appreciated. Students and trainees look up at the specialists as their role models, hence our professional attitude must reflect that.

Having gone through various stages and experiences in my

career in surgery, observing myself and all levels of medical students, postgraduate trainees and colleagues, I've come to include a very vital element of self-assessment which is well-known by the term 'reflection'.

I would always be conscious that I have given full attention to every patient I see in different clinical scenarios and be sure, as much as I can, that the patient was satisfied before leaving the outpatient clinic or before I move to the next patient on a ward round.

A time for 'reflection' always follows, simply assessing my own performance and trying to understand, for example, the reasons for what seemed to me less than full satisfaction by a certain patient and/or their relatives during the consultation. There should always be some time also at the end of any clinical session with patients, be it a clinic, ward round or post-operatively, for the student and trainee to reflect as well, and for ourselves to respond to their queries.

Of vital importance here is the service provided by the nursing staff after surgery, particularly for major and complicated operations.

The skills of performing an operation, no matter how major or complicated, can be acquired after proper training. However, one should always remember that skilled post-operative care by well-trained nursing staff is the second most vital factor for the eventual, hopefully successful outcome. My colleagues and I were always happy to explain to our surgical nurses aspects of post-operative care for different types of surgical operations, particularly the more major procedures. We were always very much encouraged by their interest and motivation to learn and improve their skills.

Among the conclusions in his paper published in 2017, Ali

R Shukor et al highlights, among other facts relevant to health care in Kurdistan, the lack of a proper system of training of the nursing staff.[36] In the same paper, Ali R Shukor highlights the impact of different barriers and conflicts over the preceding two decades on the structure and delivery of health services, both primary health care and specialist services in Kurdistan.

I was also lucky that I met with a number of Kurdish doctors in several hospitals in the UK, which was also a good opportunity to practice my Kurdish language skills.

Among them was Dr Barzo Faris Dizayee, a consultant microbiologist, and Dr Sarhang Hussain, currently a consultant colorectal surgeon in Erbil, with whom I worked for several years at TGH and the MRI.

---

[36] Ali R. Shukor et al. 'Primary care in an unstable security, humanitarian, economic and political context: The Kurdistan Region of Iraq'. BMC Health Services Research. Volume 17, Article number: 592 (2017)

CHAPTER 3

Language Barrier in Communication

I will address here what I consider one vital issue of direct communication with patients and their relatives in different clinical scenarios, whether in outpatient clinics, ward rounds, pre-operative stage and other face-to-face encounters.

I will only project my personal experience here, which I came to firmly accept as an essential element of communication with my patients and their relatives while working in Erbil. This firm belief in direct face-to-face communication and talking to my patients and their relatives, in Kurdish, was of great help to me and more so to my patients to build up an additional element of rapport, trust and confidence towards their management success.

I fully respect any different opinion from my colleagues here, not forgetting also the fact that I started working in Erbil in 1980 when I was 32 years of age and knowing that I might be working there for many years, quite likely for the rest of my surgical career.

It took me only around three to four months, early 1980, to learn the basics of the Kurdish language, mainly relevant to asking questions about health and disease and understanding the answers. I did require help, but help was readily forthcoming from all around, given the nature of work and regular daily communication with all levels of staff in the hospital as well as in the community. Besides being so vital to this element of communication with my patients, the feeling that I could speak and understand a new language was really a very delightful one.

I recall during my recent return to Erbil in November 2019, and while I was out with my great friend Kaka Jihan on the outskirts of the city, a conversation with him which brought up the issue of the importance of talking to patients directly in Kurdish language. He pleased me so much when he reminded me that he once brought a Kurdish patient, a friend of his, to my clinic in the early 1980s, and while his friend started trying to explain his complaints in Arabic I replied and carried on the rest of the consultation in Kurdish.

Do I really need to expand on the vital importance of this issue of communication with patients and their relatives in their own language?

During any form of consultation, nothing parallels the regular face-to-face and eye-to-eye contact with patients, talking their language and responding directly to their questions, facial expressions and complaints.

At the start of my career in surgery in Erbil I quickly realised that most of my Kurdish patients, particularly those coming down from rural areas, either spoke little or no Arabic at all. Most of them were accompanied by a relative who was sometimes able to translate, though I sometimes also needed the help of my secretary for translation in my private clinic.

My knowledge of the basics of the Kurdish language helped me also during my work in the last 26 years in the UK. During these years I met with a number of Kurdish patients and their families whose knowledge of English wasn't good enough for communication and they were very pleased when I spoke to them in Kurdish. Again this direct doctor–patient communication works much better than carrying out a three-way consultation with the presence of an interpreter.

CHAPTER 4

Doctor's Health

The other issue I feel vital to address here with regards to our lifelong profession is our state of health, which could surely impact adversely on our performance. Doctors, like all human beings, are susceptible to all kinds of stress, tension and diseases. As a matter of fact, their unique responsibility towards patients puts them at a much higher level of stress and tension than in most, if not all, other professions.

The General Medical Council in the UK addresses this vital issue regarding the health and wellbeing of doctors while caring for their patients during the annual appraisal process for every doctor in the UK. It's an absolute requirement that every doctor confirms to their appraiser that they are enjoying good health, both physically and mentally, and capable of carrying on with their duties and providing the expected level of healthcare to their patients.

If my mind or body is unwell for any reason, then it's obviously impossible for me to deliver the same level of care to my patients compared to when I'm enjoying my normal state of good health. We must never forget that most patients, if not all of them, can readily perceive whether the doctor is paying enough attention to them or seems to be in a hurry and rather dismissive in their attitude.

The same applies to the care delivered by the nursing staff, not forgetting that the nursing staff spends much a longer time than doctors looking after patients.

What is also vital to stress here is that, contrary to physical illness, mental stress can easily be masked behind what appears a perfectly normal behaviour by a very stressed person. This is particularly so with professionals holding high levels of responsibility, doctors in particular.

Having said that, it is no surprise then that problems with management of patients are more likely to happen when the mentally stressed medical professional is unable to devote their full attention at a time when patients need it most.

When answering complaints raised by patients or their relatives in respect to dissatisfaction with care, or the occurrence of a post-operative complication, the doctor's defence that they were tired or not feeling well that day is a very poor defence and ethically unjustified.

CHAPTER 5

Medical Education, Society and Professionalism

In the journal BMJ open, Ashton Barnett-Vanes et al wrote: 'Beyond passing exams, it is important for medical students and young doctors to understand how healthcare is provided in their country, besides understanding the cultural aspects and various health needs of their society.'[37]

On numerous occasions while working in the UK between 1976–1980, I came across patients who were so open to divulging lots of information about themselves and their family members. So, it was quite usual for one patient to tell me, for example, that his wife had breast cancer, another that one of his children was being treated for leukaemia, and yet another that he was in state of depression for one reason or another.

Surely, we all incorporate family history as an essential component for the completion of our clinical assessment of our patients and the planning of management steps. However, our patients anywhere in Iraq may understandably be reluctant to divulge certain personal and family health information, mainly due to social and cultural factors.

On the other hand, the junior doctor may not concentrate

---

[37] Ashton Barnett-Vanes, Sondus Hassounah et al. 'Impact of conflict on medical education: a cross-sectional survey of students and institutions in Iraq'. BMJ Open 2016;6:e010460.

on obtaining full family history not just because of socio-cultural factors, but also because such detailed history may not appear to be vital for gaining further useful knowledge to help manage the disease in question.

Obviously, time constraints facing doctors seeing so many patients, for example, in a hospital outpatient clinic anywhere in Iraq, as highlighted in a paper published by Goshan Karadaghi et al.,[38] makes it impossible sometimes to obtain the full relevant history about the medical condition itself, let alone a family history. This is obviously a different problem altogether with various organisational, staffing and resource issues, which need to be addressed collectively.

However, dealing with inpatients is more likely to offer the opportunity to cover all aspects of history-taking by the junior doctors.

In other words, as medical teachers we always need to instil in our students and postgraduate trainees the vital ethical principle that we are managing a patient as a whole individual, whose mind is quite often busy with common family and possibly work-related issues and concerns, and now troubled by a disease condition. Managing the disease itself in isolation from the whole patient as an individual is always missing a vital aspect of the management process.

It is not really difficult to understand or explain the reasons behind the readiness of a patient to be more forthcoming with information to their doctor. It's simply the trust and confidence that gradually builds up towards the doctor which

---

[38] Goshan Karadaghi and Chris Willott. 'Doctors as the governing body of the Kurdish health system: exploring upward and downward accountability among physicians and its influence on the adoption of coping behaviours'. Human resources for health (2015) 13:43.

makes every step of subsequent management more likely to be successful. That sort of trust and confidence by patients and their relatives depends mainly on the professional and humanistic approach of the doctor.

I realise that in most situations our communication with our patients goes smoothly without any significant problems. However, when the outcome of an intervention, especially in surgery, doesn't go according to the plan and a complication happens, then patients and relatives are very likely to be dissatisfied and make a complaint.

This is, quite often, expected and justified. Very often, however, the components of the complaint include not just the dissatisfaction with the outcome and the particular complication, but also the unhappiness and dissatisfaction with various steps of the medical care delivered by doctors, nurses, or both during the whole process of management of the patient.

During the 14 years I worked in Erbil, I am very happy to say that I gained full trust, respect and appreciation from my patients and their relatives, and hardly recall any significant issues or complaints or dissatisfaction relevant to the care delivered. I surely had my share of post-operative complications, but I'm firmly convinced that regular explanation and communication with patients and their relatives at various stages of the management process goes a long way in understanding the outcome and need for any further treatment.

In the UK, the General Medical Council (GMC) publishes annually a report on the numbers of doctors either suspended from work (for a period of 3–12 months) or erased permanently from the medical register. The report in 2014 clearly showed that the most common cause for either was 'dishonesty', which involved 19 out of 43 cases. Dishonesty is clearly taken very seriously by the GMC, not only because of the potential consequences of the dishonesty but also because of the potential impact on the public's perception of the medical profession.

Thus, dishonest behaviour constitutes a serious departure from fundamental principles of good medical practice and the standards expected of a doctor.

Inappropriate relations and behaviour of the doctor, and clinical issues (some including an element of dishonesty) accounted for the suspension or erasure of the practicing privileges of the other 33 doctors.[39]

While preparing the manuscript of this book, I managed to go through a considerable number of published research articles relevant to the delivery of medical education as well as the structure of health systems and delivery of health services in Kurdistan and Baghdad.

These articles, I firmly believe, need to be read by every doctor in Iraq to have a better and clear understanding of the difficulties facing these most humanistic targets aiming to improve various aspects of provision of health services across

---

[39] The GMC describes what is meant by 'good medical practice'. It says that as a good doctor you will:
- Make the care of your patient your first concern.
- Be competent and keep your professional knowledge and skills up to date.
- Take prompt action if you think patient safety is being compromised.
- Establish and maintain good partnerships with your patients and colleagues.
- Maintain trust in you and the profession by being open, honest and acting with integrity.

the country, as well as improving and updating the delivery of under and postgraduate medical education.

I would strongly recommend my medical colleagues and students to read a recently published research article by Riyadh Lafta et al.(11) entitled 'Perceptions, experiences and expectations of Iraqi medical students'.[40] The paper highlights that medical education, both under and postgraduate (UGME, PGME), like all other sciences, is fast progressing and advancing all over the world, offering access to a globalisation of training.

In the past few years, the number of free massive open online courseware (MOOCS) options have increased dramatically, offering the options of blended learning approaches to education in Iraq.

However, wide scale implementation of the PBL system for UGME in Iraqi medical colleges is a critical initial step. Substantial revision of the curriculum and teaching methods to shift focus to student-centred learning from the traditional lecture-based approach will go a long way to facilitate online linkages with different Western medical schools.

Mustafa Al-Shamsi published a paper entitled 'Medical Education in Iraq: issues and challenges' in the International Journal of Medical Education in 2017, highlighting the need to move from the traditional mode of teaching, which is mainly teacher-centred, to a student-centred, self-teaching style based on the principles of PBL.[41]

---

[40] Riyadh Lafta, Waleed Al-Ani, Saba Dhiaa, Megan Cherewick et al. 'Perceptions, experiences and expectations of Iraqi medical students'. BMC Medical education: 2018, Article number 53.

[41] Mustafa Al-Shamsi. 'Medical Education in Iraq: Issues and challenges'. Int J Med Educ. 2017; 8: 88-90.

A very useful research paper published in 2015 by Goshan Karadaghi and Chris Willott, referenced earlier, entitled 'Doctors are the governing body of the Kurdish Health System etc.', highlighting various difficulties facing the medical health professionals, is also strongly recommended for reading. The reader may identify more negative than positive aspects in this research article, but I believe the authors projected their observations in an honest and transparent way.

I have witnessed during my visits to Erbil in 2019 several positive steps to improving some aspects of the service, from both the educational and health service delivery points of view. The PBL system of education has already been started in the medical college. The different departments have also been adequately covered by teaching staff from both ministries of higher education and of health. There are still some elements to address, particularly with regards to the structure of delivery of health services, both as primary care and specialist services.

A famous Chinese proverb says: 'The best time to plant a tree was 20 years ago' the second-best time is now.'

I found the paper published by Namir G. Al-Tawil and Sherzad Shabu et al., entitled 'Evidence-based health policy-making in Iraqi Kurdistan. etc' extremely helpful in understanding the reasons for the difficulties in implementing the outcome of research in health policy making in Iraqi Kurdistan.[42]

---

[42] Sherzad Shabu, Namir G.Al-Tawil et al. 'Evidence-based health policymaking in Iraqi Kurdistan: Facilitators and barriers from the perspective of policymakers and advisors'. Zanco J. MedSci., Vol.19, No. (3), 2015.

CHAPTER 6

Increasing Public Awareness

Over the last two to three decades, the public has become much more critical and inquisitive about the quality of care they receive from any health institution. The availability of a wealth of knowledge on the internet has made Western society much more knowledgeable about diseases and their management.

If it is not already happening, should we not expect then that some similar change in the attitude of our society in Iraq, particularly the young generation, will happen towards the medical profession? I'm sure my experienced colleagues in Erbil and anywhere in Iraq have already witnessed that.

Patients in the UK, for example, have the right to choose the NHS hospital and the specialist they wish to be treated by. This is largely based on the presence of audit data on the internet, provided by specialists in different fields, highlighting their performance results, particularly in relation to different surgical procedures.

Every hospital in the UK makes available to the public the so-called 'patient information leaflets', which contain adequate information, in different languages and in an easily understood text, about different diseases and their management in all aspects of medicine and surgery. Basic and easily comprehended explanation of many interventional procedures, including surgical, is provided. These are free to pick up by the public and they are spread in various spaces in different primary care settings and in hospitals including clinics and wards.

Besides the educational benefits of all this, the most important aspect is to make the patient an active partner with the doctor in dealing with their health problem. The patient is more aware now of their disease condition, the options available for its management and most importantly the benefits and risks associated with any intervention.

The phrase 'Doctor, you don't need to explain too much, you know what is right for me, so just do my operation and I fully trust you', is no more valid in the UK today as I used to hear it occasionally between 1976 to 1980, particularly from elderly patients.

During my recent visits to Erbil in 2019, I was really surprised and rather upset by hearing some news about doctors, particularly surgeons, of the way they were held accountable for some post-operative complications or a mortality and how the case was eventually settled. This obviously followed a complaint made by patients or relatives.

There is a desperate and urgent need to organise and build a system resembling, to some extent at least, the medical defence societies or unions in the UK. The UK Medical Defence Union offers indemnity for clinical negligence claims and expert advice for its members. It was established in 1885 and was the first of its kind in the world.

Implementing such changes anywhere in Iraq requires significant efforts and involvement of multiple levels of institutions and authorities, not just the medical profession.

We all know that education should go hand in hand with implementing any new changes in any field in life. In medicine, this is not just limited to school education, at all levels, about health services in the country. This is surely vital, and when supported by the currently widely available knowledge on the internet, is expected to enhance public education as well.

However, in medicine, every professional has a part to play in delivering an element of education and explanation to patients and their families during direct encounters, whether in clinics, during ward rounds, peri-operative stage and at discharge and follow up. This is surely considered also as an ethical obligation.

Patients and relatives have the right to complain about what they consider a shortfall in care or a poor outcome or unexpected post-operative complication. Every hospital in the UK, whether NHS or private, has an office dedicated to listening to patients and their relatives when they decide to complain. They are named 'patient advice and liaison services' (PALS).

The process could be rather a lengthy one but the voices of the public and medical professionals are listened to carefully, followed by full analysis of the events which led to the dissatisfaction of patients or relatives. Opinion of experts in the relevant specialty of surgery, or any branch in medicine, might be sought. Patients have also the full right to take their case to the solicitors if they were not satisfied with the final local conclusion, which only happens infrequently.

Some issues, like professional misconduct and serious complications, often end up with the MDU for final decision making.

Starting in the UK in 1976, I always used to spend enough time in the clinics to explain, briefly and in simple language, to my patients and their relatives their health problem and the options to deal with it. I would very often resort to making sketches on a paper about the affected part of the body, and try to explain the problem in simple ways and how to deal with it.

Is that too much of a time to waste? Is it unnecessary because of the assumption that patients and relatives might not comprehend most of that? Or is it simply because of the time constraint whether in a busy clinic or on ward rounds?

In reality, none of that. This is my firm conviction built on my 14 years of work and clinical experience in Erbil, where one might expect the need to change such an approach because of socio-cultural differences and time constraint.

This was the period in my life and practice as a surgeon and medical teacher which made me realise that, together with skills and knowledge, proper and ethical communication with patients and their relatives is always rewarded by mutual satisfaction, trust, respect and boundless appreciation.

Surely, I encountered a number of patients and relatives, in Erbil, who were not sure why I was trying to explain, in detail, about their disease condition and the need for a particular surgical operation, making occasionally some illustrating sketches as well at the same time. I could even sense the smile on their face expressing their surprise for my indulgence in what they considered as unnecessary and rather lengthy explanation.

However, such a counselling session is never a waste of time no matter what the background of our patient is. The session will always be remembered by the patient and their relatives as reflecting the doctor's interest in their disease condition and the respect and concern for their health. That's one vital, essential bridge, helping to build trust and confidence towards the medical profession.

Today, in Western society, the public expects more from the medical profession than just good knowledge and excellent skills. This is simply because, as highlighted before, that errors, mistakes and complications will continue to happen no matter how careful and experienced the medical professionals are.

One of the main reasons for complaints by patients and/ or their relatives, as well documented by MDU periodical publications, is the poor explanation and communication with them prior to and occasionally after the occurrence of the incident or complication. The word 'dismissive attitude' is often used by the claimants in their complaints.

Conclusions and Reflections

> '**Our mind is enriched by what we receive, our heart by what we give.**'
>
> Victor Hugo

Starting my medical career after graduation in 1970 from the medical college in Mosul, I initially worked in Iraq for six years, which included my training as an SHO in surgery at the MCTH in Baghdad. This was followed by my first exposure to the practice of medicine and surgery in the UK, between 1976 to 1980. I subsequently worked in Erbil as a consultant surgeon from 1980 to the end of 1993, and as the dean of its medical college during the last four years.

Memories of the two wars, the eight year Iraq–Iran War and the First Gulf War, as well as the unfortunate internal conflicts, are full of bitter and painful experiences. In retrospect, and whenever I think back on these years, I feel also proud that, despite all these difficulties, we managed to achieve most of our goals rendering a good service to the community and maintaining an excellent standard of medical education.

This is surely the outcome of teamwork under prolonged stress and pressure. The credit goes to the service rendered by the health staff of both the university and Ministry of Health, the students, the staff of all the governmental hospitals and society.

And so, I firmly believe that the perseverance and genuine interest in work and respect of humans are best tested at times of stress, conflict and crisis.

I was promoted to the academic position of 'assistant professor in surgery' by the University of Salahuddin in Erbil in 1993.

Forced departure from Erbil in 1993 led to immigration, as a family, to Canada in 1994, followed by my return to the UK in 1995, where I had to go through three and a half years of retraining in different surgical subspecialties. After passing the exit exam I have been working as a consultant general surgeon in Manchester since the year 2000. My fields of practice, until 2013, were in colorectal, endocrine and breast surgery as well as basic laparoscopic surgery.

I was also appointed as the undergraduate tutor at Trafford General Hospital from 2002 until 2013. I have carried on working, to this day, at both Trafford General Hospital and the Manchester Royal Infirmary, following the merger.

Despite the well-organised working environment in the UK and the availability of all facilities and resources, I was sure all the time that I was offering much more needed help to my students and society in Erbil. That was always my feeling, despite the difficult times during the 14 years I worked and taught there.

A busy daily schedule, even occasionally on Fridays, with three or more operative sessions every week, combined with regular daily teaching, was never tiring, and rather enjoyable. I started working as a specialist at the age of 32 in Erbil, facing a huge load of surgical problems. I enjoyed the challenges I faced, and I knew that I was up to it, given my young age, deep love of my profession and enthusiasm. The financial aspect was never thought of as a priority or a reward for my hard work, but just to provide me and my family with a reasonable standard of living, let alone the fact that there were no opportunities or available time to dedicate to a profitable private practice.

What still stands out most in my memory today is the

expression of boundless gratitude, respect and love from my patients, previous students, currently specialists in different fields in medicine, colleagues and the society of Erbil. I can't think of any more precious prize or reward I could have received, still presented to me today by the same society 26 years later.

Whenever I recall and remember the years I worked in Erbil, with relentless dedication to my patients, students and society, I always conclude with great joy that the greatest gift of life is most genuinely felt in our loving relationship to the people around us, offering the help which we can provide.

I remain very eager to return to Erbil, even at my rather senior age, and offer any support and help needed.

There is also the magnetic beauty and the charming scenery of Iraqi Kurdistan, with breathtaking views of the hills and mountains all around you, which sticks in your mind with a feeling of deep belonging to this nature. It is no surprise then that, historically, Erbil is probably the oldest continuously inhabited city on Earth.

Verses from the Holy Koran and the Holy Bible, preaching messages of love and helping fellow man

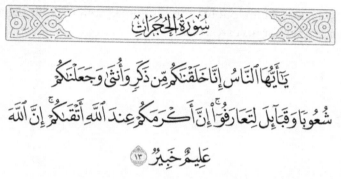

Al-Hujurat, Verse 13 (from the Holy Kuran)

In the Name of Allah, the Most Gracious, the Most Merciful

O Mankind! We have created you from a male and female and made you into nations and tribes that you may know one another. Verily, the most honourable of you with Allah is that who has Al-Taqwa.[43] Verily Allah Is All Knowing, Well Acquainted.

Luke 10 (from the Holy Bible)

Love your neighbour as yourself.

When the law expert asked 'And who is my neighbour?'; Jesus told him about the story of the 'Good Samaritan'; when a

---

[43] Al-Taqwa means being helpful, honest and a believer.

robbed wounded man was left to die on the road between Jerusalem and Jericho, and was ignored by both a Priest and a Levite who were passing by, a travelling Samaritan came to his rescue, saved him, put him on his donkey and took him to an inn, paying for his care as well.

Dr Waleed Khalid, sat in his office.

Dr Waleed Khalid

Ankara, Baghdad, 1980

The last days of the summer in 1980 were stifling hot but overshadowed by heavy rains. The streets of Ankara were witnessing heated struggles between the leftist and rightist groups, which had resulted in the deaths of many innocent people for ideological reasons. The situation was far from under control, and there was fear that the army might interfere and overtake the democratically elected government of Süleyman Demiral, which had happened previously when the army had ousted the government during the September 12 coup d'état (Turkish: 12 Eylül Darbesi), which was led by General Kenan Evren, who was the chief of the general staff at the time.

On the other hand, the conflict between Iraq and Iran was at its peak, since Ayetulla Al-Khomayni had promised that this revolution was for all of the Arab and Muslim countries. Iraqi president Saddam Hussein was preparing his army to fight against Iran. As was expected, on 22 September 1980 heavy and aggressive air strikes began against Iran, which started a war that would last for eight years. No one on either side expected that this war would continue for such a long time or cause so much destruction to both countries, not to mention killing approximately one million people, and causing various disabilities, some permanent, of hundreds of thousands.

In July of that year (1980), I was preparing to leave Ankara and go to Baghdad to start working as a board-qualified thoracic and cardiovascular surgeon, with interest in congenital heart surgery.

I was sure that my extensive experience in trauma surgery, which I had gained as a result of the daily clashes between the two sides, thus resulting in so many wounded patients being admitted to the Hacettepe University Emergency Department in Ankara, would allow me to do my best for my patients in Iraq during the war.

When I arrived in Baghdad, the situation was very tense, with the electrical power off all over the country for security reasons and the drums of war beating steadily, while the television channels were broadcasting enthusiastic songs that praised the bravery of the Iraqi soldiers.

Due to the bureaucratic requirements in Iraq, I had to wait four months for an appointment at the Ministry of Higher Education.

It was a nice opportunity for me to stay for this period of time in the small town of 'Beledruz' where I was born. Beledruz belongs to the province of 'Diyala', northeast of Baghdad, and is approximately 45 KM from the Iranian border. Time spent with my family and friends was most precious and I always recall that with a deep sense of nostalgia. We lived in a small house, and we had a nice farmland where delicious citrus fruits and dates grew every year and always had a special delicious taste compared to what we might sometimes buy from downtown.

Initially, I was appointed to the position of a consultant thoracic and cardiovascular surgeon at Salahuddin University in Erbil, to start working in 1980. However, mainly as the result of some logistic aspects related to my specialty, a period of secondment occurred for two years at the Medical City

Outskirts of Beledruz, rich in date palm trees.

Teaching Hospital in Baghdad before I began working in Erbil in the latter part of 1982.

On the first day of work at the MCTH, I went to the ninth floor, where the thoracic and cardiovascular department was located, to meet with the head of the department, Professor Dr Yousif Al-Naaman. He welcomed me and showed me all their facilities and introduced me to the other members of the staff. He was a very kind person and very hearty, God bless his soul. He was a very well-known surgeon worldwide, as well as a weightlifter.

I began taking care of my patients and was very happy to work with Professor Al-Naaman, as I sometimes assisted him. He admired this way of working as a team, since the other consultants were used to operate individually, assisted only by junior surgeons.

The days with Professor Al-Naaman were very happy days. He was very fatherly, angry at times, but very sweet as well. I miss all those days when we worked together. He was a very influential figure, not just due to his knowledge, skills and professional attitude, but also because of his love and dedication to teaching.

In addition to my routine work at the MCTH, there was a deep concern in my mind about how to build the thoracic and cardiovascular surgery unit in Erbil. I asked Professor Al-Naaman about that, and he promised to help me as much as he could, but both of us knew that it was not easy to build a new modern cardiac surgery centre in another city in Iraq.

This is due to the lack of infrastructure, in addition to the difficulties in identifying and educating the staff which is required, at a time when the country was involved in a modern and very costly war.

The cardiac centre at the MCTH in Baghdad dealt with all kinds of cardiac, thoracic and vascular surgeries. It was the first of two centres, both in Baghdad, the second of which was also actively working, and was directed by the Ministry of Health (Ibn Al-Nafis Hospital).

The MCTH was the main teaching centre for students at the medical college in Baghdad. There were two other centres in the country; one in the city of Mosul, in the north, which belonged to the University of Mosul, and the second in the city of Basra, in the south, which belonged to the University of Basra. Neither of these two centres was an active cardiac surgical centre due to the same problems, comprising a lack of facilities for open-heart technology and well-educated support staff. In other words, they only dealt with thoracic and vascular cases.

All of these circumstances were challenging, but encouraged me to do my best to start organising a good centre in Erbil, not just to serve the people of Erbil from both surgical and educational aspects, but also to have a centre in the north of the country.

However, I was quite hesitant about going to Erbil prematurely, as I was unsure about the available resources and staff for my speciality at that time. Hence, I decided to continue to work at the MCTH in Baghdad and prepare for a future in Erbil.

With regards to open-heart surgery, we were performing all types of adult and paediatric operations, but there were some problems with coronary surgery due to the lack of invasive cardiology and coronary angiography at that time.

Dr Al-Naaman and I began to prepare the list of instruments and equipment that would be necessary for thoracic and vascular surgery in Erbil. We organised a list of rigid bronchoscopy (straight, non-flexible scope) sets for adults, paediatric patients and infants. These sets were used for diagnostic and therapeutic purposes. Paediatric and infant bronchoscopy would save the lives of many children and infants who had inhaled or swallowed foreign bodies in Erbil.

The Iraq–Iran War

During the Iraq–Iran war, the Ministry of Health organised a list of the surgical teams who were going to various hospitals near the war frontlines. I was mostly involved within the Amara region, where I also organised the responsibilities and duties of the different members of my team.

The team consisted of a senior surgeon, assistant surgeon and surgical nurse. One day, when we were on our way to Amara, we heard about a brutal and ferocious battle that had occurred the previous night in the Amara region, and that many hundreds of soldiers may be on their way to the army hospital that we were going to.

The surgeon assisting me was Dr Saad Saleh Al-Mahaidi, who was very hard working, as well as very skilled. (He is now working as a consultant general surgeon at Manning hospital, Taree, Australia.)

He told me that we had to get some rest because the journey from Baghdad to Amara was quite tiring. On the first day of our week-long duty in Amara, I was lying on my bed and thinking about the long hours ahead of us, and how we could cope with such a large number of casualties. It was a difficult, vague, and unpredictable situation. Despite all these stressful moments, I felt reassured by the well-equipped hospital and qualified working personnel, which made me feel confident that we would be able to do our best for the young wounded soldiers.

Suddenly, Dr Al-Mahaidi knocked on the door, informing me of the arrival of many wounded soldiers. We all rushed down to the emergency department to start assessing them, and to deal first with the more serious ones. Meanwhile, we told the personnel to take the mattresses off the beds and put them down on the ground, in order to accommodate as many wounded as possible. Most of them were suffering from shell and high-velocity missile injuries. The X-ray queue was so crowded that we had to treat many patients with chest injuries by the insertion of drains (chest tubes) to evacuate the collected blood and allow the lungs to expand. This was obviously based on clinical diagnosis, aiming not to lose any time waiting for chest X-rays to be performed, while letting those with less severe injuries wait for proper radiological assessment.

The chest tubes were lifesaving in the majority of chest injuries, as the bleeding gradually slows down and eventually stops. The supply of blood was very efficient and rapidly provided as the staff was very well-qualified and hard working.

Much to my surprise, we were able to save the life of a soldier who sustained a shell injury to the right ventricle of his heart. This patient was bleeding profusely through his chest tube; hence, as in similar situations, I had to open his chest to control it. The shell was seen protruding through a hole in the wall of the right ventricle, with severe bleeding during relaxation of the heart muscle (diastole) and then cessation of the bleeding with contraction (systole). It was very easy to remove it and the hole was sutured using specially supported sutures.

Unfortunately, the incidence of lung blast trauma and diaphragmatic rupture were very high due to the high number of velocity missile and artillery casualties. To my surprise, there were also some wounded Iranian soldiers, and we gave them the same care as we gave the Iraqi soldiers. On the third day, the heavy clashes had somewhat declined, and we became a bit more comfortable and were able to conduct detailed examinations of the patients.

There were unwritten orders at the time that we should not report the number of wounded soldiers, which caused a problem for us, as it prevented us from submitting scientific papers to journals or international meetings. However, we were given permission to report the percentage, rather than the real number.

We continued to work with Dr Al-Mahaidi at the Amara Army Hospital for one week. After that, we handed over the task to my colleague, Dr Auff Alsamarrai, who also works in the same unit at the MCTH. We returned to Baghdad to start working on our elective cases, and the list of equipment and instruments for the future centre in Erbil.

At the same time Salahuddin University in Erbil had insisted that I join them in creating the cardiothoracic centre as well as for undergraduate education.

After completing all the steps of the bureaucratic process, in the latter part of 1982, I was ready to pack my suitcase and head to Erbil. The distance from Baghdad to Erbil was about 400 km and it took some four hours to get there.

Erbil, September 1982

Upon my arrival in Erbil, I found myself in the middle of a crowd in the streets who were protesting against the government of Baghdad and Saddam Hussein. I was very astonished by that, as it was considered very unsafe for the Iraqi people to gather in the streets and protest, because Saddam was very strong and aggressive in punishing his opponents. At that time, I realised that my work in Erbil was very likely going to involve casualties and injuries due to clashes, and not just elective cases.

After finding a house to rent, I went to the College of Medicine to meet with the dean, Dr Nawzad Alattar, who warmly welcomed me, promising to do his best to create a good thoracic and cardiovascular unit within a short time.

On my second day there, I went to see the hospital where I was going to practice as a surgeon and perform operations. I was surprised that there was nothing at the Al-Jamhouri Hospital in relation to my speciality as a thoracic and cardiovascular surgeon. Even the managerial and administrative personnel of the hospital were unaware of this.

It was a very difficult day, as I found myself alone, like a soldier who was unarmed in battle. I only had my students to give lectures to, but they were missing the clinical application, including observing and assisting in theatre, which is vital to understand fully the subject of chest surgery. I decided to drive to Baghdad to meet Dr Al-Naaman and obtain the instruments necessary to enable me to perform emergency operations, since requesting the supply of such instruments and facilities, along the formal routes of application, would have taken a much longer time.

I was successful in that and was able to obtain two sets of instruments for chest surgery, and two sets of bronchoscopy instruments of different sizes. I was very happy about that, like a small child who had received an enjoyable gift from his father.

I began my duties by admitting common cases of chest and vascular problems for surgery, sharing the general surgery ward at Al-Jamhouri Hospital in Erbil, and putting my list of operations within the lists of general surgery. I began to develop good relations with the other doctors from the surgery and medicine departments, some of whom were very keen to help me in achieving my goals in the establishment of this centre, such as Dr Farhad Huwez and Dr Amir Al-Dabbagh, the author of this book (known as Mr Al-Dabbagh in the UK, since qualified surgeons are called by this title rather than Dr, which is given to physicians). As time passed, I realised that I needed a separate ward for my own patients, having already started to train a good number of nurses and sub-staff in order to correctly handle post-operative care.

I started to persuade some of the nurses, especially those who were from Ainkawa, to work with me. At that time I began talking to Dr Abdulrazzak Al-Dabbagh, the general director of health affairs, who was very cooperative and understanding. He was also the most senior consultant general surgeon in the city with FRCS qualification from the UK.

Over time, and after performing so many successful operations, the good reputation of the unit was widely perceived, not just by the hospital staff, but also by the society of Erbil as well. Within a short period of time we started to receive patients referred from other cities like Duhok, Sulaymaniyah, Kirkuk, and even from Mosul. In addition to our elective cases, there were a great deal of causalities coming to the emergency department and requiring urgent management.

One day, Dr Abdulrazzak Al-Dabbagh told me that they had decided to give us a separate building, which was the emergency ward of Al-Jamhouri Hospital after it had been properly renovated and well-equipped.

I was so delighted with that and started to select some nurses and staff who had already been working with me. The building was on the right side just next to the main entrance of the hospital.

Every member of the team was so excited, as if he or she was wating for their new house to move to. I started to feel more confident that, with this team and I together, we were going to lay the first stone of the thoracic and cardiovascular surgery department in the region. This unit was to become a unique centre, serving patients from all around the region.

As a consultant surgeon, I was alone, and I was required to be on-call day and night to deal with all urgent civilian chest and vascular trauma, as well as any causalities from the clashes between Saddam's forces and the Peshmerga, which were taking place all over the region, and mainly occurred at night.

The situation in Erbil was a bit tense and the city was unsafe, especially during the night. As a result of that, they used to send an ambulance with a police escort to pick up the doctors in the event of an emergency. However, this resulted in a waste of time that was considered a gold standard for life-saving in urgent cases.

The distance between the hospital and the village of Zanco, where I was living, was around five kilometres. The village of Zanco was a very modern complex that consisted of nearly 90 houses, which were built by a European company, each on a 400 m2 plot of land, with front and back yards. There was a good market and very nice preschool for children who were under six years of age. The disadvantages of these nice houses were that bullets and high-velocity missiles could penetrate the walls; hence, it became very dangerous to live there due to the heavy internal clashes, as well as bombings by the Iranian aircrafts, which started to happen later. To protect my family, I decided to make a shelter after consulting my brother Faiz, who was an officer in the army at that time, as this was before his death during the war. We dug into the ground and built an L-shaped shelter in the back yard.

A Telephone Line in My House, a 'Miracle'

Another problem that we faced in the village of Zanco was its distance from the hospital and the lack of telephone communication, due to the absence of a network. However, I was successful in connecting a special long line, which was the only telephone in the village.

The story regarding my telephone line was very strange and happened by chance. You see, I had applied to connect a telephone line to my house several times but was unsuccessful. The city's telephone communication officials claimed that it was not possible, due to the long distance and the absence of telephone columns in the region of the village.

Once, at midnight, there was a knock on my door by the police officers, who were accompanied by some people that I did not recognise at that time. They introduced themselves as members of the Baath party, who were the main leaders of

Erbil, and informed me that there had been heavy clashes between them and the Peshmerga, and there were many wounded soldiers. In addition to that, one of the leaders of the Peshmerga was wounded and needed urgent treatment, since it was vital to get some important information from him.

When I got to the emergency department there were several VIPs surrounded by their armed guards, in addition to important city officials, including the general director of telephone lines, as well as the Baath party leader of Erbil, whose name was Waleed. He was very polite and open-minded person, who had ordered the others to leave the room and let me deal with the wounded patients.

I began with a wounded patient from Peshmerga, who was surprisingly very relaxed and happy to see me, and I had realised that he might have heard about me. I presented myself to him and informed him that he had a penetrating wound to the lung that could be treated easily by the insertion of chest tube. I instructed the resident to prepare several pints of blood just in case they were needed. He did very well. Then, I moved onto the other wounded patients, and everything went very smoothly.

I felt that this was a good time to bring up my telephone problem, explaining to them that I was the only chest surgeon in Erbil, dealing with all of these emergencies, but I had no telephone in my house. Then, I noticed that their leader (Waleed) turned to the general director of telephones and said to him, 'Tomorrow at 12 noon I will call Dr Waleed (which was my name at that time on my Iraqi identifications), and if there is no connection I will put you in jail.'

I was very happy as the line was connected and became functional before 12 noon the following day.

That day I had a meeting with the staff and residents, and informed them that I now had a telephone, so I did not need to be escorted by ambulance or police, as they could now just call me and I would drive to the hospital soon after that, as required.

On the other hand, it was a tricky situation for me to be the only telephone owner in a village of 90 houses, as it was difficult to turn back requests from neighbours to make phone calls now and then.

The Birth of the First Cardiothoracic and Vascular Unit in Erbil

The restoration and upgrading of our new unit had come to its end. There was a nice operating room and a small ward with some rooms that we could use as a post-op intensive care unit.

First cardiothoracic vascular unit.

We stuck a note at the entry of the building, clearly stating: Thoracic and Cardiovascular Surgery Unit. By sticking up this note we had announced the birth of the unit, and now I really appreciated the effort and dedication of all of people who had worked with me to create this unit, which was to be remembered by future generations as the first thoracic and cardiovascular surgery unit in the region.

We started an intensive educational program for the nurses regarding the post-operative care of patients. Here, I had to remember all of my colleagues from the medical and surgical departments who had helped us to achieve such a successful outcome. The first generation of nurses, who were trained properly, began to teach the others during the following years. The people of Erbil spoke Kurdish, local Turkish, as well as Arabic. They were very peaceful and respectful towards the doctors, especially anyone who was not from Erbil, due to their hospitality towards guests. They were very under-standing and believed that the doctors were doing their best to treat and save the patients.

During my stay in Erbil, for more than eight years, there were never any complaints made by patients or their relatives, or any negative incidents with regards to myself or my team, and I never witnessed any disrespectful behaviour. Such a positive professional relationship always motivated me and my team to work harder, building an atmosphere of full trust and respect by my patients and society over the years I worked there. After my settlement in Ankara in 1992, I kept receiving patients from Erbil, some referred by previous medical colleagues, and others coming directly for management of their problems.

Scope of My Work in Erbil, Fully Enjoyed, but Frustrating

The chest and vascular procedures had become routine work with good results, due to the well-trained anaesthetists and nurses. As time passed, I realised that this type of work was very tiring, and that I needed well-trained surgeons to share the task with me.

Inhaled and swallowed foreign bodies were such common and serious occurrences among infants and small children, and it was always a source of great delight to everyone to see them recovering nicely following endoscopic intervention and removal of the foreign object.

In addition, the other hospital which needed my services for emergency cases, including war casualties and some elective cases, was the army hospital in Erbil. That was where Erbil International Airport is standing today. I was surely happy to help them.

I also fully enjoyed my educational commitments to my students, which happened almost every day.

In spite of my busy work, I was deeply unsatisfied by the fact that I had, unavoidably, drifted away from my main speciality of adult cardiac surgery and congenital heart surgery. It was quite difficult to persuade the people in power to support me in that, because their main concern was the war with Iran as it was very costly, and their only aim was to focus on treating the young soldiers.

The Opening of Rizgari Hospital 1984–1985

As time passed and 1985 approached, we all began to prepare ourselves to move to the new hospital, which was very well-equipped and had an excellent operating theatre complex. The hospital was built by a Japanese company named Marubini. It was a unique hospital for this region with a very well-equipped intensive care unit. The operating theatre complex was controlled by a central station with broadcasting screens from all theatres, providing real-time transmission to the lecture hall, in the ground floor for the medical students.

In 1985, we left the thoracic and cardiovascular surgery unit at Al-Jamhouri Hospital and moved to the newly built Rizgari Hospital, called 'Saddam Hospital' at that time. Our first unit became a 'neurosurgical unit', headed by the neurosurgeon Dr Mohammad Ali Tawfiq.

Rizgari Hospital was very well-furnished and equipped, and we were able to perform surgery on the day of our transfer. The director of health affairs had asked me to run the intensive care unit with my nursing team, which was an opportunity that allowed me to manage more complicated cases in the new hospital. The intensive care unit had six beds and one separate room used for septic cases.

This was another task that I had to handle, in addition to the routine and emergency thoracic and vascular surgery cases.

The Al-Jamhouri Hospital continued to function normally, catering for both medical and surgical elective and emergency admissions. In addition, there were separate paediatric and maternity hospitals.

In retrospect, I as well as my team always felt nostalgic

towards our previous and first cardiovascular and thoracic surgery unit, since it held a special place in our hearts.

During my work at A-Jamhouri hospital, I met with an enthusiastic general practitioner who was working in the emergency department, Dr Nawzad yahya Bajger, who expressed his interest to join me for training and practicing in the thoracic and cardiovascular surgery unit, to which I agreed, and so we started working together. He was a nice man, motivated and supportive to the plan of constructing the unit.

This unit served for three years, at which time we relocated to the Rizgari (Saddam) Hospital, as mentioned previously.

Due to the escalating aggression of the Iraq–Iran war, we were advised to carry on with our regular clinical commitments, and to postpone the open-heart surgery project because of the difficulties in securing the vital infrastructure.

One of the VIP managers had told me one day, 'With the money that you intend to spend on open heart surgery, we could buy four tanks and one mirage aircraft, so please try to save our brave soldiers first.'

At that time, I had realised that I was still far away from my dream regarding open-heart surgery. I decided to see the reality of Iraq, which taught me to do my best for my patients, my students and to be more realistic with what I had in hand.[44]

---

[44] In our first unit at the Al Jamhouri Hospital, we were able to start dealing with some heart problems applying the techniques used in closed-heart operations, such as opening of the stenotic mitral valve (a valve in the left side of the heart), peeling of the heart wall for diseased stiff walls of the heart (pericardiectomy), and some congenital heart diseases, such as patent ductus arteriosus (PDA), which is persistence of a narrow communication between the aorta and the main lung artery.

I was very happy that we had such well-trained anaesthetists (Dr Mahmoud Jasim and Dr Hameed Al-Dabbagh and Dr Mohammad Thabit), so that we could continue to perform more complicated cases, both elective and emergency.

In addition to my routine surgeries, I recognised that the incidence of oesophageal cancer was very high in the region, so Dr Amir Al-Dabbagh (the author of this book) and I decided to devote some of our time to perform surgery for this disease, with good results, along with our dear friend, Dr Hassan Al-Naqshbandi, who was the first to perform oesophageal surgery.

I continued to work in the region as the only thoracic and cardiovascular surgeon, which was tiring, but it made me happy to feel that I was doing something for people from all origins, without knowing their ethnic, political or religious backgrounds, and being a role model to the students, who would be the future doctors after our departure.

The most beautiful feeling in life is to see your students carrying forward a sacred message and knowing that you had a role in that. All of this filled me with joy and serenity, but I must also confess that I was 32 years old, which is a golden age for surgeons.

The salary was low and there was little time to deal with the private clinic due to the unexpected rush of emergency cases, day and night, which mostly comprised of children with inhaled foreign bodies, civilian war casualties, in addition to road traffic accidents and internal conflicts. I am not telling all these stories to make myself appear as a hero, but so that the younger generations will remember that and learn the important lesson: 'Remember the past to know how better to build the future.'

As a result of working this way, and when finances were not an issue between us and the patients, there was the gradual build-up of mutual feelings of trust, respect and full confidence by patients and society towards our genuine interest in helping them. That sort of atmosphere was very well appreciated and learnt by our students.

The hospital provided an ideal environment for education on all levels, and the medical students were very happy witnessing and experiencing the benefits of all that. Mr Amir Al-Dabbagh became the dean of the medical college, in addition to his clinical commitments and active daily bedside teaching. In addition to that, Mr Hassan Naqshbandi began to create a modern gastro-intestinal endoscopy unit after receiving good training in Japan for six months.

There was a good scientific environment and we worked as a team, helping and even assisting each other, without thinking about financial profit.

The consultant physicians, Dr Hama Najhim and Dr Meriwan N Omar started performing flexible bronchoscopy, which was very important in providing early diagnosis of lung diseases, guiding surgical management when indicated.

I continued to perform rigid bronchoscopy as a therapeutic procedure for removal of foreign bodies from the tracheo-bronchial tree and oesophagus.

With the continuation of the Iraqi–Iran war on the fighting fronts, including the northern sector, there was another duty, which was treating those with chest and vascular trauma. In addition to the military casualties, there was a number of civilians who were injured due to the Iranian air strikes.

The military casualties were admitted to the army hospital in Erbil, while the civilians were admitted to the emergency department at Al-Jamhouri Hospital. The simple vascular cases were handled by the army general and orthopaedic surgeons, but they called me when necessary, and I was ready to help them whenever they called. I was also on the list of on-call surgeons to go to Sulaymaniyah Hospital, a major city in Kurdistan, Iraq some 150 kilometres to the east of Erbil, to treat the wounded soldiers following battles of the Iraq–Iran war, on the Gardamand sector along the front-zone in the north-west.

The war lasted for eight years and the surgeons in Iraq did learn a lot from it with regards to surgical trauma management, much like the experience gained by surgeons during the Second World War and other wars.

One day, when I was in Sulaymaniyah, we received many casualties from the war zone. There was a long line of patients who were wating for surgical treatment, and I was very surprised when I saw a soldier with a traumatic leg amputation who was accusing another soldier with leg amputation of stealing his leg for reimplantation. There were so many tragic events during the war, witnessed frequently by surgeons and their staff.

As the work at Rizgari Hospital was going very well with the elective patients, we were also taking care of civilian and war injuries in our daily practice, and although the medical and surgical staff worked very hard, everyone was also worried about their families due to the continuous bombing by Iranian aircrafts and the high incidence of civilian casualties. The bombing usually took place in the early morning, and everyone considered themselves a possible casualty due to the inaccurate targeting of the bombing sites, which might have been valid for the Iranian targets on the other side as well.

Blast trauma and injuries from high-velocity missiles were difficult to recognise, unlike the civilian trauma and stabbing wounds, where the affected organs could easily be identified.

One day, one of the Iranian bombers targeted Rizgari Hospital, which unfortunately hit the intensive care unit at 8 o'clock in the morning. I was on my way to the hospital, so I was able to get there very quickly to treat the injured patients as well as our staff. It was terrible to see such a hospital being targeted.

The shelter at my house, in the village of Zanco was used by my family and neighbours, and became the safest place to rush to once the siren was heard. I had no choice at such times but to prepare myself to rush to the emergency department once the second siren, indicating end of the air raid, was heard.

Compulsory Military Training of University Staff, July-October 1986

During such a period of heavy responsibility, we, as university staff, along with all university students, were ordered to take part in four months of military training in the Dibbis region near Kirkuk. The order was from Saddam himself, and nobody could refuse or even think about not obeying such an order. My concern was about the casualties who had vascular and thoracic injuries, as well as my elective patients in Erbil. No one could dare tell the higher officers that it was risky to leave Erbil Province without a thoracic surgeon at a time when the war was at its peak in the northern front-zone.

Dr Amir Al-Dabbagh, Dr Fadhil Abbas and I attended the military training together on a very hot day in Dibbis. The

165

evening of that day was very dark, and we went to the camp store to receive our bedding and military clothing. We were told to sleep as early as possible, because we had to get up at 6 o'clock to stand in the long queue for the morning soup prior to the early morning training.

The large, long hall was full of university professors, but my bed was side-by-side with those of Dr Amir Al-Dabbagh and Dr Fadhil. The month of July 1986 was extremely hot, and the training was very exhausting for all of us. They treated us as new trainee soldiers, side-by-side with our students. No one was given permission to leave the camp.

The training lasted for four months, and we returned to the university and hospitals to continue where we left off.

During the final years of the war, the air strikes intensified on both sides, associated with long-range missiles targeting the major cities, which was frightening everyone due to the unpredictability of the targets. The majority were fatal because of the blast-wave trauma, which increased the incidence of lung complications and respiratory distress syndrome. The demolished buildings and people trapped under the rubble also created a difficult situation, causing acute renal failure and crush ischemia of the extremities and muscular necrosis. In such situations, the seriously wounded civilians often required a team of surgeons from different specialties to deal with injuries of multiple organs.

In August of 1988, the war ended when a ceasefire was agreed to on both sides. Everybody was very happy to hear about that and to return to a normal life and safe daily activities.

The war left behind great losses, with more than a million deaths but no clear figures regarding numbers of disabilities, probably a few hundreds of thousands. The financial costs were estimated at 350 billion dollars. The families on both sides felt bitter relief, as large numbers of them had lost members as well in the war, besides being unsure about the future with such a massive economic loss.

The dream of establishing an open-heart centre was, unfortunately, far from being realistic, as everyone was working on emergency and urgent cases.

After the end of war in August 1988, I was hoping that the time was suitable to revisit my dream of opening an open-heart surgery centre in Erbil. However, once again, I felt alone, as the centre needed strong political support, which was not forthcoming. Having said that, some of the authorities in Erbil had promised to help in creating the centre in Rizgari Hospital. Their promise to help me made me more optimistic, but unfortunately things happened differently, and new conflict began between Iraq and Kuwait over oil and border issues. These strange and unexpected developments progressed rapidly to the point of no return. Everybody prayed that there would be no more wars, recalling the tragedies of the Iraqi–Iranian war.

The First Gulf War, January 1991

On the 2 August 1990, Iraqi TV broadcasted enthusiastic songs with the news that the Iraqi army had entered Kuwait to occupy and annex it to the governorate of Basra as an Iraqi judiciary. Again, everyone started to feel frightened and terrified, preparing themselves and their families for a new war, not knowing what would happen to the people or the country, which had hardly recovered yet from the devastating effects of the recent war.

For me, it was in vain to talk or even to think about the possibility of creating an open-heart unit while everyone was preparing for a new war. Saddam Hussein defied United Nations Security Council demands to withdraw from Kuwait by the 16 January 1991, and the Gulf War began with a massive US-led air offensive known as 'Operation Desert Storm'. This war was expected by every Iraqi and the health authorities began an intensive program so the doctors and medical staff could learn how to protect themselves from the chemical and biological weapons, and to take some measures against the atomic weapons.

There were also rumours that the major cities could be targets of mass destructive weapons if Saddam tried to use them against his enemies. Everyone started to cover their windows with nylon paper to protect their homes from the medical or biological weapons. They also gave us gas masks to use if needed.

Mr Amir Al-Dabbagh and I realised that we had to keep our families away from Erbil, so we took them to a hotel in the Shaqlawa district to keep them safe.

On the 17 January 1991 the war started. The fear of the use of weapons of mass destruction filled our hearts, but the fear of the unknown was even greater. At midnight on the 17 January, I was very restless and could not close my eyes. I tried to sleep but it was impossible, listening to the news, while beside me was the gas mask. I was frightened when I heard on my small radio that Operation Desert Storm had begun. I was alone at home. All of a sudden, I found myself wearing the mask, which was very uncomfortable. I decided to go out to see what the weather was like and what was going on outside. I laughed at myself as I saw the birds flying happily, so I took off the mask and started to breathe the fresh air.

I sat in the yard at my house, looking at the sky, as if I was waiting to see what was coming for us. The electricity was cut off, so I stayed in darkness, apart from the light from the stars. I heard then that the USA and their allies had targeted all the electrical power stations; thus, Iraq was without proper electricity for a long time, which unfortunately is still the situation today.

Advanced military technology was used by the USA and their allies, including stealth bombers, cruise missiles, so-called 'smart' bombs with lasers-guidance systems, and infrared night-bombing equipment. The Iraqi air force was either destroyed early on or was not able to fight. Unlike the Iranian bombing, we did not see the aircrafts in the sky, we only saw the rockets hitting their targets, which were mainly the electrical power stations, telecommunication centres, and other targets.

The fear by the people at that time was that such strikes might have been aimed at hidden stores of chemical or biological weapons. For that reason, they preferred to move, with their families, to the countryside and small villages to protect themselves from the dangerous air pollution that might happen, or so they thought. However, we did not experience such events during the First Gulf War, which lasted for 42 days, and comprised relentless attacks by the allied coalition, both in the air and on the ground.

One cannot forget those dark nights and terrible days that the Iraqi people suffered. We depended mainly on the generators at the hospitals, and even used candles sometimes to perform chest tube insertions, vascular repairs and thoracotomies. Then we started to suffer from the severe consequences of the sanctions which were imposed on all aspects of daily life, even the medical sector, unlike in the Iraq–Iran war when everything was available, especially the requirements for the health services.

I either forgot or neglected my plans for the open-heart surgery centre, realising it was no more a priority under the relevant conditions and instability of the war. The bulk of my work without open-heart surgery was still massive, being the only surgeon with my very busy specialty in the city.

Removal of inhaled foreign bodies in small children was my favourite work, which made me and the families very happy because we saw immediate recovery in small children who had been suffocating. Such procedures were very useful for the medical students as well, because they could see bronchial anatomy and learn the intubation and anaesthetic aspects, and medications used. As a sign of gratitude of many families, I was invited, by some, to visit them in their houses outside Erbil. This gave me the delightful opportunity to enjoy the sightseeing of many charming areas in Kurdistan, the beauty of the scenic mountains and the breathtaking waterfalls.

Such short vacations or picnics were not risk-free, due to the bloody clashes that were taking place between the Peshmerga and the government forces. We were always escorted by armed men, just like bodyguards, on our way to the invitation, which was sometimes in villages far away from Erbil. Although doctors were not a target during these clashes, the problem of being caught up between such clashes was always a risk as unintentional targets and could be hit by stray bullets. In addition to enjoying the scenery and the genuine friendship, we also had the opportunity to become familiar with the morals and customs of society there, which was very important for us as doctors serving in the region. Enjoying such social activities, Amir Al-Dabbagh and I were able to cultivate good relations and unforgettable memories that still live in our hearts today, and we both still miss those days, recalling such a kind, loyal and generous community, which we served.

As the war continued, it was clear that there were no weapons of mass destruction, which made us feel more relaxed and carried on working, returning gradually to bit more of a normal life. However, the heavy sanctions and the destruction of the infrastructure in Iraq made daily life, as well as performing medical duties, very difficult due to the lack of electricity and other facilities. None of the telecommunications worked and the operating theatres were dark, with only the light of the candles and the peak power of the hospital's generators. In addition to this, there was a lack of petrol for the cars or even the ambulances.

As life became more and more difficult, stories began to circulate about movement by the Peshmerga to occupy the major cities and expel the government forces, and there was a fierce battle between the two parties, which meant that many soldiers might be on their way to the hospital. As time passed, we began to hear the battles approaching the city. As the walls of our pretty houses were not resistant to bullets or shrapnel, we decided to retreat to the shelter that I had built in the back yard, but within a short time, the shelter was full and there was not even room for me.

I waited outside the shelter for the ambulance. However, a four-wheel-drive vehicle full of armed Peshmerga arrived earlier, and their commander, who was both a friend and an old patient of mine, told me that we had to go to the hospital as soon as possible with them. While driving fast to the hospital, we were hearing bullets fired from time to time. He told me that some of the government's forces were still fighting, but the majority had already fled to Mosul, though there were still some of them hiding somewhere in Erbil.

We started to treat all the wounded patients without having any knowledge about their background, respecting their rights. We remained committed to the medical oath by treating all patients equally, as we were blind to their peculiarities and private background, leaving the court to decide who was innocent and who was guilty.

The situation regarding daily life was so hard due to the doubled sanctions, comprising the US sanctions and those by the central government in Baghdad. After the withdrawal of the government forces and the entry of the Peshmerga into the cities, there were, unfortunately, some people who appeared to plunder and burn the government departments, even involving looting of some of the hospital facilities. Fortunately, it only lasted for a short time and then the Peshmerga forces took control of the situation. I remember at that time seeing something very funny. When I was on my way to the hospital there was a very old woman who was carrying two big, important books, Surgery of the Chest, which was written by Gibbon, and The Heart, which was written by Hurst. I persuaded her to sell me the books for a pittance and took them back to the Medical School Library.

The majority of our work around that time was traumatology at the Al-Jamhouri Hospital. It took some time before we could start to perform the less urgent cases, as well as dealing with the complications of vascular trauma and wound infections for those who were late to arrive to the hospital.

Fleeing from Iraq to Iran, and Turkey, April 1991

Day-by-day life became harder and more tense since there were rumours that the government's forces were approaching Erbil, and there would be a threat on everyone's life. Every family started to think about themselves and their children, searching for ways to get out of Erbil. I had discussed this matter with Amir Al-Dabbagh, and we decided leave to by car since we had stored two tanks of petrol at the beginning of the war if there was a need to suddenly escape from the city.

As the government's forces were approaching Erbil, the Peshmerga forces were trying to calm the people down and prevent them from leaving.

Amir Al-Dabbagh and I were at the control point to leave Erbil, realising that we were the only two families leaving at that time. We were escorted also by a dear friend, called Salah Al-Deen Shafi. Luckily, the control point officers allowed us to move on, mainly due to their deep respect to doctors.

By midnight we had arrived at Salahuddin resort to get some rest and see what was going on in Erbil, which was about 25 KM away. At that time, people trying to leave Erbil had to pass through Salahuddin resort, then through the small town of Shaqlawa, and then to Hag Omran, which is the last point on the Iraqi border, heading to Iran. Some preferred to go through the northern border, passing the rugged mountains into Turkey, but it was very difficult and dangerous for small children to go walking about in such rugged terrain.

As we departed, we started to hear the sound of artillery fire and helicopters on the road between Erbil and Salahuddin resort, resulting in many casualties and deaths. Our travel plans comprised going to Iran by car, and then from Iran to Turkey, where we would live and work. After passing the Iranian borders, they took us to the security department, and after deep interrogation of each of one of us, we went on to a camp in the town of Khoy, which was close to the Turkish–Azerbaijan border. By our second day in Khoy, the camp was full of people coming from Iraq and it became very crowded, so much so that unavoidable long queues took place to get the things that we needed. Our kids became very disappointed as they had expectations of a luxury vacation after fleeing Iraq.

It was very hard to tolerate those days in the camp. After several days, the director of the camp told us that we could go to Urmia, but we had to work, unpaid, in a hospital that was receiving wounded patients from Iraq. It was a very happy day when we got out of the camp and stayed in a relatively comfortable hotel in Urmia. Our families were very happy about that, and Amir Al-Dabbagh and I started to visit the hospital where wounded Iraqi were admitted. Apart from traffic jams, Urmia is very nice, clean city and the drive to the hospital was comfortable, with stunning views all around. A friend of mine, an Iranian doctor who studied and qualified in Turkey around the same time that I qualified, came to visit us in the hotel and offered to help, asking us if there was anything they could do. They were nice people, who owned very nice houses with charming yards. The standard of living indoors was very modern and we spent unforgettable days in Urmia. We were grateful to all of them for their kindness and hospitality as it made those very difficult days easier to tolerate, and were even a bit enjoyable.

I managed to meet the with the Turkish counsellor in Urmia, who knew that my wife was Turkish and was very kind to help us to get into Turkey, crossing the borders to the city of Van on the Turkish side. We stayed in Van for one night and then headed to Ankara early the following morning. I learnt, sometime later, that Amir Al-Dabbagh and his family returned to Erbil a few weeks after I entered Turkey.

Ankara had changed a lot and had become more modern, clean and very well-organised and enjoyable to live in. It was the first time in 11 years that we had lived somewhere without the sound of war and weapons being fired, but the effects of the trauma of war remained with my three daughters, and it took some months for them to learn to cope with the sounds of the Turkish civilian airplanes as a result of their fear of the possibility of bombings, having been preconditioned for that in Erbil.

In October of 1991, I joined the medical college of Gazi University in Ankara, and participated in all types of cardiac surgeries, in addition to vascular operations.

In 1995, I was successful in my aim to pass the examination for associate professorship, and after working hard at both surgery and teaching, I was able to attain professorship in cardiovascular surgery in April of 2002.

In 2006, the staff members of the department of cardio-vascular surgery unanimously elected me as the head of the department. It was a great opportunity for me to refresh my skills in paediatric and infant cardiac surgery as well as training young surgeons, who are currently performing all types of infant and paediatric heart surgeries all over Turkey. I was so proud of that and became even happier when I saw them performing the more complicated cases better than me. When I saw my students performing operations so successfully, I felt pride in the job that I had done as their teacher.

Today, when I recall the past, I think about what I have achieved at Gazi University, it makes me think about what went wrong in Iraq and why I was unable to achieve the same things there in a country known, historically, to be the cradle of civilisation and later the richest country in the world.

It was not until December of 2007 that open-heart surgery emerged in Erbil, and the local government opened a heart centre and heart surgery. Dr Imad Ahmad Jamal and Dr Mohammad Mahmoud Saleem were the first to perform early open-heart surgery in Erbil.

My dream of an open-heart surgery centre had finally come true and I was very happy to hear that, appreciating the amazing efforts of everyone who had helped to fulfil my dream of creating an open-heart centre, which we were not able to achieve during the 1980s due to the wars, conflicts and lack of stability.

At the present time there are so many centres in Erbil, Sulaymaniyah and even in Duhok that perform open-heart surgery, and they really do a great job. Until the opening of the Open-Heart Surgery Centre in Erbil, most of the patients came to me for heart operations or went to Iran or Jordan. After the opening of the first centre, it became easier to open others, since the first centre also became a centre of education for the sub-staff, which was vital to start with. In developing countries, qualified sub-staff and manpower are more difficult to find. I had faced such difficulties when I started working in

Erbil, and it was difficult to find the people who would work harder for the same salary. The second dilemma that the heart surgeons in Iraq faced was related to the short working hours, as every doctor was rushing to go to his own private clinic in the afternoons.

With such short working hours, it would be very hard to perform a second operation in one theatre, so the number of operated patients would be very limited and the wating list would become very long, which might result in unpredictable heart complications due to a delay in proper treatment.

When Amir Al-Dabbagh asked me to write a chapter in his book, I gladly accepted, realising that our times of hard work, teaching and perseverance to achieve the best successful outcomes were rewarded by the happy satisfaction and successful progress of our medical students and by the genuine respect and appreciation of the society in Erbil. This, happily, has remained alive in their memories to this day.

Laying down the first stone for cardiothoracic and vascular surgery unit in Erbil was difficult and needed a lot of effort. I still feel very lucky that I have been able to help a society that was so deserving of it.

Introduction to the author

Graduated with MBChB from medical college in Mosul, Iraq in 1970

Fellow of the Royal College of Surgeons of Edinburgh (FRCS Ed) 1978

Fellow of the Royal College of Surgeons of England (FRCS Eng) 1979

Consultant General Surgeon and Clinical Lecturer in Erbil 1980–1993

Dean of the medical college, Erbil, University of Salahuddin 1989–1993

Associate Professor of Surgery, medical college, Erbil 1992.

Fellow of the Royal College of Surgeons of Edinburgh (FRCS Ed, Gen. Surg.), 2000, following further postgraduate training and passing the 'exit exam'

Undergraduate Tutor at Trafford General Hospital, Manchester, England 2002–2013

Awarded Best Clinician of the Year 2013, at Trafford General Hospital.

Published five articles in surgical journals, three of which were in international journals

Published eight case reports in international journals

CPSIA information can be obtained
at www.ICGtesting.com
Printed in the USA
LVHW082001261121
704543LV00009B/109

9 781789 632453